912

# KENT
# OUR COUNTY

by

## H. R. PRATT BOORMAN
C.B.E., M.A., F.J.I., D.L.

1979

KENT MESSENGER
NEW HYTHE LANE, LARKFIELD,
KENT, ENGLAND

ISBN 0 900893 11 7

Printed in Great Britain by Headley Brothers Ltd The Invicta Press Ashford Kent and London

# FOREWORD

Kent is a prosperous County; we are lucky to live here and to enjoy it. Oh yes, of course we grumble—that is an Englishman's privilege—and we take for granted all the good things we enjoy here. But should we?

The winter of 1978/79 was abominable. Kent was stated to be the worst hit County. During January snow blocked the roads, especially at Lenham, and between Dover and Deal. Cars were abandoned and drivers were urged to stop at home. Even the sea was frozen at Pegwell Bay.

That was not all. Ambulance men went on strike on January 22; so did the public services, including the refuse collectors. The only railway running on January 16, 1979, in Britain was the Romney, Hythe and Dymchurch Light Railway, which daily takes students to school and home again.

But when the sun comes out in Spring and the fields become green once more, Kent returns to The Garden of England, and we all feel better.

Owing to the prosperity and growth of our population and industry, we are fast losing some of our Garden of England, known by this name ever since Kent sent its green produce, apples and potatoes to the City of London. Sadly most of our cherry trees have now gone, due to picking difficulties. We miss their beauty in the Spring, but our apple orchards are increasing and there are also the strawberries, currants, raspberries and flowers, and so many other things grown in the fertile soil of The Garden of England.

Today we enjoy "picking our own" strawberries, and even rhubarb, especially if we are able to do it in short shifts.

We miss the cheerful humour of the London hop-pickers, who used to come down to Kent in their thousands with their babies and prams, and even curtains to decorate their hopper huts. Today the bines are taken to the oast-houses by tractor, and the hops picked by machine.

Most of our farming is done by tractors and milking-machines. The combine has taken away the toil of cutting, stooking, loading and thrashing our crops.

Electricity, too, has reduced much of the hard work, both in our homes and on the farms, due to the growth of our power stations at Dungeness, Kingsnorth and Pegwell Bay.

Industry has grown. Papermaking is going well, and more of the pulp for paper is grown in our woods, and the North Downs will supply chalk for our cement works for many years to come.

Our towns are healthy and prosperous and are growing fast with new estates and industry. The growth of the tourist trade is spectacular. Ferries from Dover, Folkestone, Ramsgate and Sheerness are carrying passengers, cars and container lorries in greater and greater numbers across the Channel, bringing back food to our people and tourists willing to spend their wealth in our County and Country. Eight and a half million passengers passed through Dover alone in 1978; 1,800,000 through Folkestone; and 500,000 through Sheerness.

Tragically the proposed Channel Tunnel has been held up, but despite the continued improvements in our ports it is still wanted, especially for export trade.

The Duke and Duchess of Kent have taken a keen interest in our County. The Duke opened the new St Peter's Bridge at Maidstone in 1978.

Princess Anne and her husband have competed in riding competitions at the Kent Agricultural Show and at Knowlton. Princess Anne and Princess Margaret have inaugurated hovercraft from our shores, and have taken part in many other visits.

We are so glad that HRH Prince Charles, The Prince of Wales, has already taken up residence at Chevening Place. He has accepted the Freedom of the City of Canterbury, visited our County Police Headquarters at Maidstone, and planted a tree at his residence as Patron of the Men of the Trees.

We are also pleased that HM Queen Elizabeth, The Queen Mother, has accepted the invitation to be the first lady Lord Warden of the Cinque Ports. During the informal procession after her installation at Dover Priory, she could not help breaking ranks to talk to the people, especially the children and senior citizens. Her smile and charm brought happiness everywhere she went.

We always have a rousing welcome for Her Majesty The Queen and for the Duke of Edinburgh whenever they visit Kent. They have paid many visits, including Canterbury Cathedral and the Royal British Legion Village, and at times have visited the village of Mersham privately where Prince Philip has enjoyed shoots and has played cricket.

Kent is a loyal County and we welcome these opportunities to express our loyalty.

Many other events are referred to in this book. The enthronement of the 101st Archbishop of Canterbury, Dr Donald Coggan, who in addition to his ecclesiastical duties is interested in meeting people and seeing where they work. He and his wife have visited the "Kent Messenger," the County Paper of Kent. We are all so sorry that he is due to retire in January 1980, but glad he will still be with us and live at Sissinghurst in Kent.

We regret the retirement of Lord Cornwallis, KCVO, KBE, MC, who has served Kent so well all his life, and is known as the "Spirit of Kent." He still receives "Kentish Fire" at the many functions he attends. When he retired as Lord Lieutenant of our County on July 31, 1972, The Queen appointed Lord Astor of Hever, whom we welcome. We thank both him and Lady Astor for their devotion to our County.

Perhaps the most important duty Lord Astor has carried out on behalf of Her Majesty so far, was to present to Ashford its Royal Charter, a day which Ashford's third mayor, Councillor Harry Watts, so rightly referred to as a "momentous occasion in Ashford's history."

Yes, Kent is an historic and prosperous County. We are proud of our geographical position, which brings us in close contact with the other nations of Europe.

\* \* \*

I wish to express my grateful thanks to all those who have helped me in the preparation of this book; to the members of the staff of the "Kent Messenger" and "Kentish Express", to the Invicta Press, and to all my friends.

St Augustine's Priory, Bilsington.                                  H. R. Pratt Boorman.

HM Queen Elizabeth, The Queen Mother, who accepted the invitation to be the first lady Lord Warden of the Cinque Ports, was installed at Dover Priory on August 1, 1979.

Let the dunes and the Downs sound and echo
And the beacons illumine the sky;
The turbulent sea be tranquil,
And safe the ships that pass by.
The lights of Dungeness flash their message,
All clear, good cheer and safe passage,
From harbour, past headland, by haven to Dover:
Old Ports in the Channel to 'half sea over'
As Hastings and Sandwich, Romney and Hythe,
Winchelsea, Rye, 'Antient Towns' with the five,
And those forgotten ashes of history's embers
Their corporate and incorporate members:
All this landlocked and maritime cordon,
Rejoice at the choice, and with one common voice
Acclaim their well-loved Royal Warden.
For a presence that graces the Courts
Now presides over Shepway and Ports.
May all 'live under the pleasant yoke'
The Warden brings to the Cinque Port folk.
England, passant, gules, guardant, or,
Demi-hulls argent, emblazoned, azure:
Their ancient, heraldic banner they raise,
To welcome their Warden; to wish Happy Days!

Edward Body.

3

Her Majesty's Yacht, Britannia, arrives under the White Cliffs in Dover Harbour, bringing HM Queen Elizabeth, the Queen Mother, on July 31, 1979.

The Queen Mother is welcomed ashore by Lord Astor of Hever, Lord Lieutenant of Kent.

The Queen Mother arrives in a semi-State landau at Dover Castle, of which she is Constable, with a 60-strong escort of Household Cavalry. With her are Prince Edward, Viscount Linley and Lady Sarah Armstrong-Jones.

During the procession at Dover Priory, the Queen Mother was accompanied by Councillor Mrs Betty Wells, the Speaker of the Cinque Ports and Mayor of New Romney.

The Queen Mother took time to chat with children at Dover Castle and also with senior citizens, patients of the Royal Victoria Day Hospital. Her charm brought happiness wherever she went.

The Queen Mother went to St Mary's Church with Brigadier Maurice Atherton, the Deputy Constable of Dover Castle, accompanied by Prince Edward.

The Queen Mother inspected the Guard of Honour of Naval personnel outside the Maison Dieu, Dover's Town Hall, during gusty weather.

HRH The Duchess of Kent opened the new YMCA and Church Institute "Y" Sports Centre in Maidstone, in May 1967. She is seen arriving at the Sports Centre with the Mayor of Maidstone (Mrs W. Goodchild) and Lord and Lady Cornwallis. Mr T. Scholes, the Town Clerk, is on the right.

County Hall and offices were erected in 1915 in the forecourt of the Sessions House at a cost of £50,000. They were designed by Mr F. W. Ruck, the County Architect, and are built of Kentish ragstone, faced with Portland stone. Judges try cases in the Maidstone Crown Court here.

The Church of All Saints is a splendid building, striking in size and symmetry. It was founded in the Perpendicular style together with the College by Archbishop Courtenay, under King Richard II. It is believed to be on or near the site of the original St Mary's Church. The tower originally had a steeple 80 feet high, which was struck by lightning on November 2, 1730. The College was suppressed in King Henry VIII's reign.

It was decided to build a Town Hall in Middle Row, High Street, Maidstone, suitable for the use of the Mayor and Corporation in 1758, on land which had been used by the Council for some time. The public subscribed to the cost and the County gave £560 in order that the Hall could be used by the Kent Assizes and for County business, too. The Police Court was below and the Town Council meetings were held in the Hall above. The Town Hall was extended in 1853. In 1937 the Police Court moved to Palace Avenue.

HRH The Duke of Kent unveiled a plaque and cut the tape to open St Peter's Bridge, an additional bridge over the River Medway in Maidstone, Kent's County Town, on Thursday, November 23, 1978.

The £2.5 million St Peter's Bridge at Maidstone, 61 metres long, was handed over to the Kent County Council and received by the chairman, Mr Alistair Lawton. The Duke of Kent (the first royal visitor to lunch in County Hall) was on the platform with Lord Astor, Her Majesty's Lord Lieutenant, and the Mayor and Mayoress of Maidstone (Councillor and Mrs John Wood). The bridge was dedicated by the Bishop of Maidstone, the Right Rev Richard Third. The Chairman of the County Council referred to "the high degree of co-operation between the Maidstone Council and the Kent County Council".

The Mayor of Maidstone, Councillor John Wood, is given a scroll for presentation to the Duke, commemorating the opening of the new bridge, by the president of the Chamber of Commerce, Mr Derek Powell, and Mr T. Carpenter, branch chairman of the National Federation of Self Employed and Small Businesses.

Mr Arthur Thatcher, the Registrar General, opened Maidstone's new Register Office at Stoneborough House, King Street, on September 13, 1978, expressing the hope that many long and happy marriages would take place there. Mr Thatcher was welcomed by the Chairman of the Kent County Council, Mr Alistair Lawton; the Mayor of Maidstone, Councillor John Wood; and Councillor David Davis, Chairman of Tonbridge and Malling Council.

The Maidstone Town Library in St Faith's Street was opened in 1964. It has a central lending library with about 76,000 volumes, a reference library, and a children's library, as well as a newsroom and rooms for meetings.

Mote Park, Maidstone, is a delightful park in which many forms of sport take place, including cricket, football and yachting. Here we see the start of the senior English Schools' cross-country race on Saturday, March 18, 1978.

Fishing, too, is a relaxing pastime on the lake in Mote Park.

HRH The Prince of Wales opened the Communications and Operations Centre in the Kent County Constabulary Headquarters at Maidstone, and unveiled a plaque commemorating his visit, on April 25, 1977. Chief Constable Barry Pain was presented to him by Lord Astor of Hever, the Lord Lieutenant of Kent.

During the afternoon Chief Constable Pain presented the Prince with a mounted truncheon, recalling his visit to the County Police Headquarters.

Lord Cornwallis, Lord Lieutenant of Kent (from 1944 to 1972), presented on behalf of The Queen, the Queen's Award to Industry, to Mr G. R. P. Leschallas, chairman of Messrs W. & R. Balston Ltd., on July 15, 1968.

Soxhlet Thimbles, used for chemical extraction and air filtration, being made at Springfield Mill, Maidstone.

Ever since Penenden Heath, Maidstone, was the scene of the trial between Archbishop Lanfranc and Odo, Bishop of Bayeux, who was accused and convicted of taking lands and privileges belonging to the See of Canterbury, Maidstone has been the County centre for trials.

Great ceremony takes place when the Judges visit the County Town, for the Judge represents the Sovereign. Here a fanfare is sounded by musicians Gary Rossiter (left) and Richard Porter, as Mr Justice Thesiger arrives at the Old Palace, Maidstone, to go to All Saints Church. He was welcomed in 1978 by the Mayor of Maidstone, Councillor John Wood. The mace bearers, Laurie Winter (left) and Arthur Avery, head the Council procession from the Old Palace to All Saints Church.

The Mayor and Council, headed by the mace bearers, and Judges proceed from the Old Palace to All Saints Church, Maidstone.

Mr Justice Thesiger and the Mayor of Maidstone, wearing full Mayoral robes and chain, chat before the Church service.

The Mayor introduces members of the Maidstone Town Council to the Judges. Mr Justice Thesiger speaks to Councillor Emil Marchesi.

The High Sheriff of Kent, 1979–80, Mr John Shipton, leaves the Judges' Lodgings near Maidstone with Mr Justice Francis Purchas (left) and Mr Justice John Stocker, for the Crown Court at Maidstone in July 1979.

An innovation in March 1979 of the Judges' visit was a Kent County Police Band fanfare heralding the Judges' arrival at Maidstone Crown Court, sounded by Pc Chris Norris, from Sevenoaks (left), and Pc David Banks of Ashford.

Mr Justice Stocker and Mr Justice Kilner Brown pause in acknowledgement of the fanfare, while the High Sheriff, Major Ion Calvocoressi, salutes.

During HM The Queen's visit to Preston Hall, Royal British Legion Village, on December 5, 1975, she unveiled a plaque recording her visit during the Royal British Legion's 50th anniversary year, and is seen shaking hands with the national chairman, Mr Charles Busby.

Already thousands of poppies were being made and packed in the poppy factory ready for the next Poppy Day. The Queen saw them being prepared and chatted with the packers.

The Queen also visited the fancy goods factory and the signs department, where road signs are made. She was given a real welcome by the children, when she visited the flats in Duchess of Kent Court in Royal British Legion Village.

HRH Prince Philip asked Geoffrey Steel and Ewart Austin of the North Kent Battalion Boys Brigade, West Malling contingent, what they were cooking, when he visited Buckmore Park, Chatham, in 1970.

The Lord Taverners' trophy was presented by Prince Philip to Alan Ealham, captain of the Kent County Cricket Team, at Buckingham Palace, after Kent had won the Schweppes' County Championship in 1978.

British Asians, who were expelled from Uganda, were provided with accommodation in the disused air station at West Malling in September 1972. "Welcome" was on the mat when Prince Philip paid them a visit in November 1972.

The Prime Minister, Mrs Margaret Thatcher, opened the Kent County Council Supplies Centre at West Malling in 1978, when she was Leader of the Opposition. Mrs Thatcher unveiled a plaque commemorating the opening of the centre, and was presented with a Kent emblem from the County Council.

Maidstone is renowned as a paper-making centre. Handmade paper has been made at Hayle Mill, Tovil, since 1810. A mould is immersed in a vat of "stuff" (of which paper is made), the surplus water is drained off and, with an acquired shake to interlock the fibres, the paper is formed. The framed web is then laid on a felt which, with further webs on felts, is put under the press to remove more water.

24

The paper is then dried and the sheets glazed and counted.

Mr Edward Heath opened the new "Kent Messenger" works at New Hythe Lane, Larkfield, and started up the new rotary press, before a large company on January 19, 1970, shortly before he became Prime Minister on June 18, 1970.

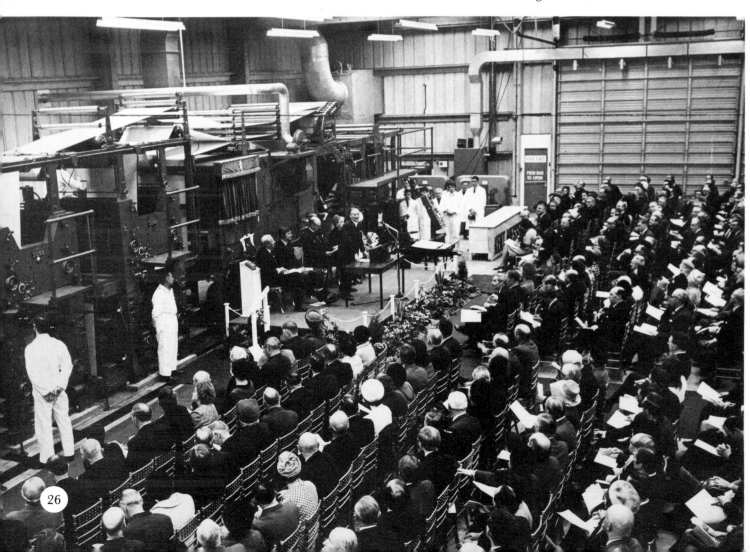

Lord Astor of Hever, Lord Lieutenant of Kent, opened the Editorial offices of the "Kent Messenger" at New Hythe Lane, Larkfield, on December 1, 1972. (left to right) Messrs M. J. Finley, Jim Thompson, Edwin Boorman, Lord and Lady Astor of Hever, Mr & Mrs H. R. Pratt Boorman, and the late Mr F. T. Coulton.

Dr Coggan, the Archbishop of Canterbury, visited the "Kent Messenger" on January 8, 1979, and was particularly interested in the modern methods of newspaper production, with the help of the silicon chip. He is standing in the foyer amongst pictures of himself taken by "Kent Messenger" photographers, with (left to right) Mr M. J. Finley, Mr & Mrs H. R. Pratt Boorman, Mr J. C. Thompson, and the Rev David Painter, the Archbishop's chaplain.

The Duke and Duchess of Kent came to the Kent County Agricultural Show on July 11, 1968, and were met by the President, Lord Cornwallis, and Mr Stanley Blow. They drove round the show and up Churchill Avenue, where the Duke planted a Blenheim Oak given by the Kent Men of the Trees in memory of Sir Winston Churchill; and the Duchess planted another on the opposite side of the road. Here they met Mr Ben Tompsett and Mrs Peggy Stevens, who presented the Duchess with a book called "Glory of the Trees".

A coaching marathon was held around the arena at the annual Kent Agricultural Show at Detling, near Maidstone.

Agricultural workers who received Long Service Awards from Lord Cornwallis in 1978. Left to right: Mr J. F. Simmons of Tonbridge, 29 years' service; Mr George Beer of Canterbury, 51 years; Mr T. W. Simmons of Tonbridge, 47 years; Mr Percival Stanford of Canterbury, 47 years; Lord Cornwallis, Mr J. F. Twyman of Canterbury, 31 years; Mrs Esther Hill of Tonbridge, 44 years; and Mr Thomas Gasson of Tonbridge, 41 years.

HRH Princess Anne, on The Queen's horse "Goodwill", competed in jumping and dressage at the Kent Agricultural Show at Detling in 1974. Captain Mark Phillips was on "Great Ovation" and had a clear round in the jumping competition. He was in good form in the dressage section, too.

Captain and Mrs Phillips (Princess Anne) watch the other competitors at the Show. Princess Anne proudly wears the Union Jack showing she represented Britain at the Olympics in Canada.

Mrs Peggy Stevens presented the shield for the best three carcasses prepared for the continental market, to the winner, Mr Trevor Richards of Lacton Manor, Westwell, at the County Show in 1978. Left, is the judge from Belgium, M. Lonhienne Marc. Mr Richards also received the cup for the best Champion Romney Ram in the show.

The Duke of Gloucester meets the Mayor of Maidstone, Councillor R. W. Woods and Mrs Woods, at the Golden Jubilee of the Kent Agricultural Show in 1979, before he presents the silver gilt 50th anniversary medals to the champion livestock breeders, and the long service medals. Lord Falmouth, the Chairman, is on the right.

In 1979 the Duke of Gloucester planted a tree at the Golden Jubilee Kent Agricultural Show, and chatted with the Archbishop of Canterbury, Dr Coggan.

Can you drink a yard of ale? Efforts to do so caused a lot of fun at the Kent County Agricultural Show.

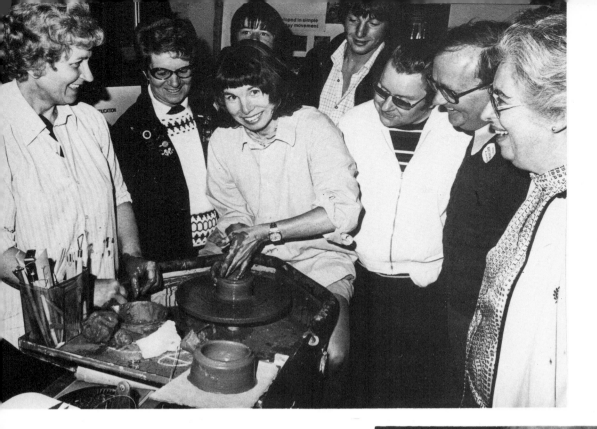

Members of the Tonbridge Adult Education Centre in the KCC tent at the Kent Agricultural Show, demonstrate their skill at the pottery turntable.

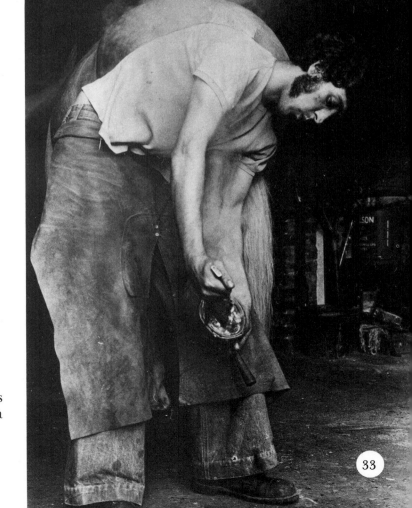

Trevor Stern of Yalding shows his skill as a blacksmith champion by shoeing a horse.

Believed to be the most beautiful castle in the world, Leeds Castle, near Maidstone, stands in the middle of a lake, formed by the River Len. Duke William, after the Battle of Hastings, gave the castle to his cousin, Hamon de Crevecoeur. It became after King Edward I's death, the castle of the Queens of England. It is said that the wife of King Henry V, Catherine de Valois, fell in love with the Clerk of her Wardrobe, Owen Tudor, and that their son, Edmund, Earl of Richmond, was father of King Henry VII; and so the Tudors came to the English throne.

The castle as seen from the Porter's Lodge.

HRH Princess Margaret arrived by helicopter to meet 1,000 guests at Leeds Castle in June 1979. Amongst them were Lord and Lady Astor, and the Duchess of Argyll. Katie Boyle compered the fashion show which was held to raise funds for the Dockland Settlement Trust.

Many a Queen of England has used this room in Leeds Castle for her bedroom.

The drawing-room in the castle.
Leeds Castle was bought in 1926 by the Hon Lady Baillie, who during her life spent large sums of money repairing it, and on her death left it for use by physicians and scientists. It may be used for conferences of the EEC. The American Secretary of State, Mr Cyrus Vance, used it for the conference between the Israeli and Egyptian ministers in July 1978, because of its peace and security.

King Henry VIII's banqueting hall in Leeds Castle, near Maidstone, with its tapestries. There is a 75-ft table with a top made from one oak tree.

The fireplace in the banqueting hall.

38   The village of Ulcombe celebrated Queen Victoria's Diamond Jubilee in 1897 by a comprehensive picture of the characters who lived in and loved the village. It was published by Mr E. Penstone. Why should not other villages do the same?

Lenham is a large and well-built village, often referred to, of old, as "Town Lenham". In 804 Cenulf, King of Mercia, and Cudred, King of Kent, gave West Lenham to Wernod, Abbot of St Augustine's, Canterbury. This is noted in the Domesday survey. The charter for a market was given by King John; Edward III confirmed it, and granted a fair on the Feast of St Augustine.

Lenham has a pleasant Square noted for its pageants and carnivals. The market took place in the Square.

The Lock-Up in Faversham Road, Lenham, was useful no doubt on Market days.

39

HRH Princess Alexandra opened the Queen Elizabeth School at Faversham on May 16, 1968 and chatted with many of the pupils.

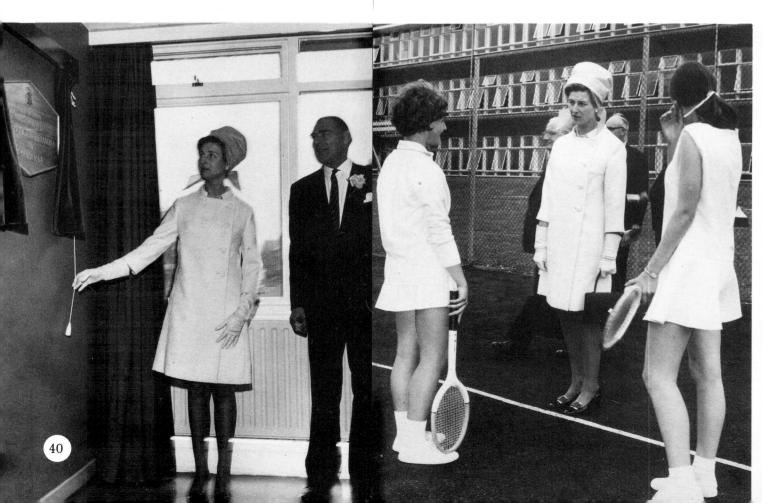

About 300 people, including Lord Fisher of Lambeth; Commander D. S. E. Thompson (chairman of the Kent County Council); Prince and Princess Andrew Romanoff; and many Kent Mayors; gathered on the lawns of Belmont Park on July 30, 1968, to congratulate Lord and Lady Harris on their Golden Wedding. Lord Cornwallis presented to Lady Harris a set of gold ear-rings, necklace and bracelet, and to Lord Harris a cheque on behalf of their many Freemason friends.

Faversham converted the 15th-century "The Fleur de Lis" in Preston Street into a Heritage Centre, which was opened by Lord and Lady Astor of Hever in March 1977. It is believed that in this inn was hatched the plot to kill Thomas Arden, Mayor of Faversham in 1547. The murder was carried out in 1551 in his home, 80 Abbey Street, and was documented in a play "Arden of Faversham".

The Pilgrims' view of the magnificent Canterbury Cathedral as they enter Christ Church Gateway.

"There is no church, no place, in the kingdom . . . that is so closely associated with the history of our country as Canterbury Cathedral."

Dean Stanley.

Queen Elizabeth II met boys of King's School, Canterbury, when she spent four hours looking at the carved stone and windows being repaired in Canterbury Cathedral in December 1976. Andrew Stein, of Ashford, told her that King's School had broken up for Christmas the day before, but the boys came back for her visit and to sing in the choir.

Celia Pilkington, the six-year-old daughter of the headmaster of King's School, presented a bouquet to Her Majesty, who was with the Dean, the Very Rev Victor de Waal.

Prince Charles took the salute at the March Past after inspecting the Guard of Honour of the 3rd Battalion, The Queen's Regiment, when he received the Freedom of the City of Canterbury at the Guildhall in 1978.

The presentation was made by the Mayor, Councillor Richard Peard, on behalf of the Council.

Prince Philip, Duke of Edinburgh, read the lesson at the 25th annual service of the Disabled Drivers Association at Canterbury Cathedral on June 25, 1978. He was welcomed by the Archbishop of Canterbury, Dr Coggan. With him were Lord Astor of Hever, the Lord Lieutenant; the mayor, Councillor Dick Peard; and the City's chief executive, Mr Christopher Gay. Ramps were placed in the Cathedral to enable those in wheelchairs to attend the service.

When Dr Coggan, the Archbishop of Canterbury, opened the 141-mile North Downs Way from Dover to Farnham in Surrey in 1978, he led the field on the Wye and Crundale Downs.

Dr Coggan, the Archbishop, enjoys a chat with Princess Anne as he takes her from the Palace to the Cathedral during her visit to Kent University in 1975.

The Prince of Wales and Princess Margaret were accompanied by the Lord Lieutenant, Lord Astor of Hever, when they went to the Cathedral for the Enthronement of the Archbishop, Dr Donald Coggan, in 1975.

The Civic procession passing through the nave of Canterbury Cathedral, headed by the Mayor and Corporation, the Kent University, and the Mayors and Barons of the Cinque Ports, at the Archbishop's enthronement in 1975.

The Archbishop, after knocking for admission at the West Door of Canterbury Cathedral, proceeds to the High Altar during the Enthronement ceremony on January 24, 1975. He was enthroned twice, first in the choir, then in St Augustine's Chair on the steps in the nave.

The Archbishop, Dr Coggan, speaks from the Archbishop's throne. During the Enthronement ceremony the Book of the Canterbury Gospels, written in the 11th century, was carried through the nave by the Master of Corpus Christi College, Cambridge.

The Archbishop, Dr Donald Coggan, at the High Altar before giving the Blessing after the Enthronement. There were 3500 people present, including the Roman Catholic Archbishop of Southwark, Dr Cyril Cowderoy and three cardinals; also leaders of the Church of Scotland and the Free Church Federal Council.

Archbishop Dr Donald Coggan, the 101st Archbishop of Canterbury, invited the Lambeth Conference to Kent in 1978. The conference was held at Kent University, with special services in Canterbury Cathedral. An innovation included in addition a conference of the Bishops' wives, arranged by Mrs Coggan, at Christ Church College. Previously the conferences had been held at 10-year intervals at Lambeth and at Church House, Westminster. Over 400 Bishops attended from all parts of the world.

Sadly Dr Coggan is due to retire in January 1980, but we are glad he and his wife will continue to live in Kent.

The south-west porch, entrance to Canterbury Cathedral. During the 1939–45 war, bombs fell in the Precincts, and the Cathedral Library, with its valuable books, was demolished, but the Cathedral escaped serious injury. King Richard I came here to give thanks "to God and St Thomas" after his release from captivity in Germany.

The magnificent columns of the nave of Canterbury Cathedral with its fan roof.

The story of Archbishop Thomas à Becket's death on December 29 at five o'clock in the evening in 1170 is shown in the Cathedral windows. How the four knights of King Henry II followed the Archbishop into the Cathedral calling out "Where is the traitor Thomas Becket?"; "I am here, not a traitor but a priest of God," was the Primate's reply. They tried to drag him from the Cathedral but he resisted, so they struck him down with their swords. The spot where he died is marked. All Europe was shocked at the violence. Because it took place inside the Cathedral and was subject to Church law, the knights were excommunicated and no other penalty was exacted. But the martyrdom and canonisation made Becket's shrine one of the most frequented in Europe.

High Mass was celebrated in the Precincts of Canterbury Cathedral by 10,000 Roman Catholics on July 9, 1970, to commemorate the 800th anniversary of the martyrdom of Archbishop Thomas à Becket.

St Martin's Church, Canterbury, where Christian worship has been offered without a break since Saxon times, was the church of Queen Bertha, wife of King Ethelbert, who was converted to Christianity in 597.

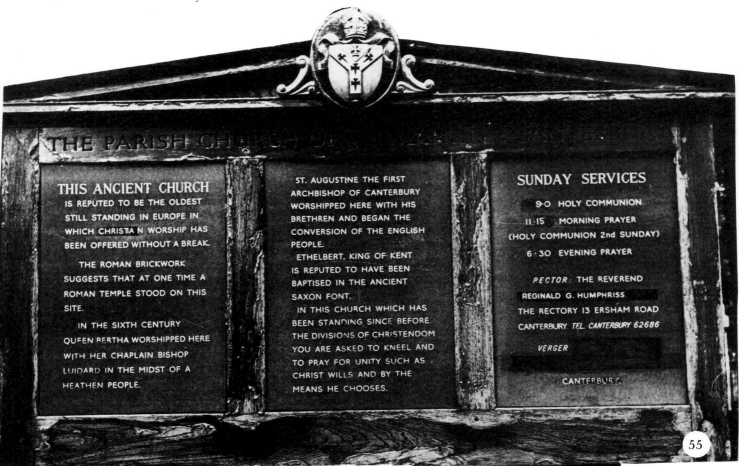

THE PARISH CHURCH

**THIS ANCIENT CHURCH**
IS REPUTED TO BE THE OLDEST STILL STANDING IN EUROPE IN WHICH CHRISTIAN WORSHIP HAS BEEN OFFERED WITHOUT A BREAK.

THE ROMAN BRICKWORK SUGGESTS THAT AT ONE TIME A ROMAN TEMPLE STOOD ON THIS SITE.

IN THE SIXTH CENTURY QUEEN BERTHA WORSHIPPED HERE WITH HER CHAPLAIN BISHOP LUIDARD IN THE MIDST OF A HEATHEN PEOPLE.

ST. AUGUSTINE THE FIRST ARCHBISHOP OF CANTERBURY WORSHIPPED HERE WITH HIS BRETHREN AND BEGAN THE CONVERSION OF THE ENGLISH PEOPLE.

ETHELBERT, KING OF KENT IS REPUTED TO HAVE BEEN BAPTISED IN THE ANCIENT SAXON FONT.

IN THIS CHURCH WHICH HAS BEEN STANDING SINCE BEFORE THE DIVISIONS OF CHRISTENDOM YOU ARE ASKED TO KNEEL AND TO PRAY FOR UNITY SUCH AS CHRIST WILLS AND BY THE MEANS HE CHOOSES.

**SUNDAY SERVICES**

9·0 HOLY COMMUNION
11·15 MORNING PRAYER
(HOLY COMMUNION 2nd SUNDAY)
6·30 EVENING PRAYER

*RECTOR:* THE REVEREND
REGINALD G. HUMPHRISS
THE RECTORY 13 ERSHAM ROAD
CANTERBURY *TEL. CANTERBURY 62686*

*VERGER*

CANTERBURY

The Greyfriars in Canterbury badly needed repair after enemy bombing in 1942, so the Dean and Chapter took it under their care. The Friars were known as Franciscans. They were mendicants living on alms and professing wilful poverty.

The Marlowe Theatre at Canterbury is named after Christopher Marlowe, the Kentish poet and dramatist, whose 400th anniversary was celebrated in 1964. There is a monument in Dane John, and also another in the ruined tower of St George's Church, Canterbury, which was unveiled on the anniversary. A banquet was held at which the Mayor, Dean, Headmaster of King's School, as well as the Master of Corpus Christi, Cambridge, and representatives of the Kent County Society, were present. A recital of Elizabethan music was also given by the Marlowe Society in the Chapter House of the Cathedral. Christopher Marlowe was the author of Faustus, Tamburlaine the Great, the Jew of Malta, Edward the Second, and many other plays.

The Weavers, where the Walloons from the Netherlands settled and showed the English how to weave silk, cotton and woollen goods. Queen Elizabeth I in 1568 gave them permission to worship in the Undercroft of the Cathedral. It is still a Huguenot Chapel. In Charles II's reign there were 126 Master weavers in Canterbury.

The River Stour passes under St Thomas' Hospital at Canterbury, which was founded about 15 years after the martyrdom of St Thomas à Becket, to house some of the pilgrims who came to visit his shrine in Canterbury Cathedral.

Kent won the County Cricket Championship in September 1970 after playing Surrey at the Oval. Kent's popular captain was Colin Cowdrey. To celebrate, the team was entertained by the Prime Minister, Mr Edward Heath, at No 10 Downing Street.
(standing, left to right) L. Kilby (masseur), R. Woolmer, J. Shepherd, A. Brown, N. Graham, J. Dye, G. Johnson, Asif Iqbal, J. Page and C. Lewis (scorer).
(seated) D. Nicholls, A. Knott (wicket-keeper), D. Underwood, M. Denness, C. Cowdrey (captain), L. Ames (secretary), S. Leary, B. Luckhurst and A. Ealham.

There's another "four" for Kent. Colin Cowdrey in action.

Another boundary! The Kent captain, Alan Ealham, in action at Canterbury in 1978. Born in Ashford, his aggressive batting is a great attraction to Kent's supporters.

1978 was quite a year for Alan Ealham. In his first season as Kent captain, he led the side to both the Schweppes Championship, and the Benson and Hedges Cup. The victorious Kent team (left to right): John Shepherd, Grahame Clinton, Charles Rowe, Chris Tavare, Asif Iqbal, Graham Johnson, Alan Ealham (captain), Bob Woolmer, Colin Page (manager), Nick Kemp, Paul Downton, Kevin Jarvis; (front left) Derek Underwood; (front right) Chris Cowdrey.

St Augustine's College, Canterbury, was the first monastery to be founded in England. It was dedicated to St Peter and St Paul, and later to St Augustine. As the Central College of the Anglican Communion, it receives priests from all over the world and seeks to play its part in reunion and the Ecumenical Movement.

The Fryndon Gate or Great Gate of St Augustine's College. The room above, with its medieval fireplace, has been used by Queen Elizabeth I, King Charles I, and also King Charles II.

The Rt Hon J. Grimond, MP, was installed on July 10, 1970, Chancellor of the University of Kent at Canterbury, when he received a Doctorate of Civil Law. With him is the Pro-Chancellor, Lord Cornwallis.

Princess Anne enjoyed her visit to Kent University when she was in Canterbury in 1975; so did those who accompanied her. She is seen coming from the Cornwallis Building.

The Pavilion of Herne Bay Pier caught fire and burnt
out on June 12, 1970. It cost £50,000 when it was built
in 1898 and the pier was the second longest in Britain
(after Southend), built to cater for the visitors on the
hoys and the paddle steamers. This Pavilion is replaced
by a £1,000,000 entertainment and sports centre, but
this, too, was badly damaged by the January gales of
1979.

The clock tower on Herne Bay promenade. On the
building is a tablet "erected by public subscription to
commemorate the services of those who volunteered
from Herne Bay district for the South African War,
1899–1902".

"As did the Few,
May the young
Who left this nest
Fly free for ever."

Outside the headquarters of the Royal Air Force at Manston a Spitfire, TB752, is displayed, which has recently been refurbished by the Medway Branch of the Aeronautical Society. It is a Mark 16 clipped wing low-flying plane for devastating attacks. Since the war it has been displayed at Manston, and during this time many birds have nested in it. One of these nests is shown on a shield with the above inscription.

A short distance away a Javelin and Typhoon, also used in the 1939–1945 war, stand on display, together, with an actual bomb used as a collecting box for the funds of the RAF Benevolent Association. A mile or so away is the headquarters of Invicta International, who also have permission to use the runways.

Kent's position, jutting into the sea, where the North Sea meets the Straits of Dover at the mouth of the River Thames, makes it a first class holiday centre. However, nothing protects it against the North Sea gales. So it happened in January 1978 that Margate lost its 100-years-old pier in a 70 mile an hour gale. The lifeboat station still remained, although it became separated from the pier. There have been several efforts to blow up the remains of the pier.

The Margate lifeboat was launched from the Pier boathouse, to go to the rescue of a vessel in one of the most crowded sea areas in the world.

Margate Pier as it was before the damage by storms in 1978.

During the ceremony of "Blessing the Seas" in January 1978, the Archbishop of the Greek Orthodox Church, the Lord Bishop of Thyateria of Great Britain, casts a Crucifix into the sea at Margate in memory of Christ's baptism. The Crucifix is retrieved by a young swimmer.

Princess Anne (Mrs Mark Phillips) is welcomed by Lieutenant Colonel L. M. Dale, chairman of the Bromley and Beckenham Branch of the Save the Children Fund, which runs Fairfield House School for deprived children at Broadstairs. When she visited it in 1974, she unveiled a plaque in the school's new gymnasium and watched the children give a display.

The Broadstairs Branch of the Dickens Fellowship holds a Dickens' Festival in June each year. They remember that Charles Dickens referred to Broadstairs as "Our little English watering place". During the week many Dickensians can be seen wearing Victorian costumes, and in 1979 the Croydon Histrionic Society presented "A Tale of Two Cities" in the Council Chamber, Pierremont Hall. There were also walks down the High Street, a Victorian cricket match, the Festival Play, "Pickwick" in Hilderstone Hall, a Victorian Musical Festival, garden parties, a Victorian bathing party, and a coach tour to Canterbury, all making a very happy Dickensian Week.

A Sergeant of the Police meets his Victorian counterpart.

"Do you remember . . .?" Just a short chat about earlier years.

The Pickwick Coach calls at the Albion Hotel, Broadstairs.

When the Prime Minister, Mr Edward Heath, visited Broadstairs in August 1972, he opened the new village hall at St Peter's, where he had learned to play the church organ. He was also present at Pierremont Hall when a bust of himself, sculptured by Mr Bainbridge Copnall, was presented to the Broadstairs Council by the people of Broadstairs. Afterwards he witnessed his racing yacht "Morning Cloud" come in second in an event organised by the Royal Temple Yacht Club. Mr W. J. E. Hammond, the Chairman of the Council is with him and Mr Bainbridge Copnall.

Mr Heath often sings as he conducts both the choir and audience at his annual carol concerts.

Full of smiles, Mr Edward Heath gets everyone to sing heartily during the Carol Service at Broadstairs.

Ethelbert, King of Kent, met St Augustine and his 40 monks here at Ebbsfleet in AD 596.

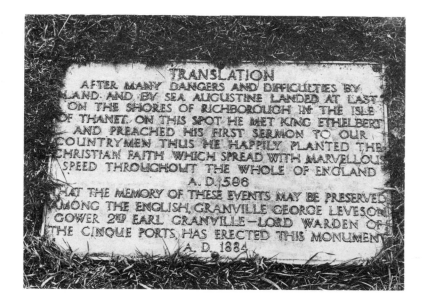

TRANSLATION

AFTER MANY DANGERS AND DIFFICULTIES BY LAND AND BY SEA AUGUSTINE LANDED AT LAST ON THE SHORES OF RICHBOROUGH IN THE ISLE OF THANET. ON THIS SPOT HE MET KING ETHELBERT AND PREACHED HIS FIRST SERMON TO OUR COUNTRYMEN THUS HE HAPPILY PLANTED THE CHRISTIAN FAITH WHICH SPREAD WITH MARVELLOUS SPEED THROUGHOUT THE WHOLE OF ENGLAND A.D. 596

THAT THE MEMORY OF THESE EVENTS MAY BE PRESERVED AMONG THE ENGLISH, GRANVILLE GEORGE LEVESON GOWER 2ND EARL GRANVILLE—LORD WARDEN OF THE CINQUE PORTS HAS ERECTED THIS MONUMENT A.D. 1884

Ramsgate was originally a fishing village, subject to St Lawrence and to the Cinque Port, Sandwich. It grew rapidly and was separated from St Lawrence by Act of Parliament in 1826. King George IV on September 25, 1821, embarked for Hanover, returning on November 8, and was so pleased with his reception and the help and loyalty shown in Thanet, that he directed that Ramsgate should in future be called a Royal Port. It is also a Limb of the Cinque Port of Sandwich. The Marina is in Ramsgate Harbour today.

Hoverlloyd 2005 arrives at Pegwell Bay Hoverport, Ramsgate, after crossing the Channel from Calais. In the background are the three cooling towers of Richborough Power Station.

Sandwich Guildhall was erected in 1599. It has an actual example of "empanelling the jury", for the jury box is set in a wall and is accessible only by moving a panel.

At the time of the Saxons, Sandwich was known as the most famous of the English ports. There were many foreign raids; indeed, the Danes captured the town. In 1450 the town walls were built to protect it. They are now a promenade. There were five gates, of which only the Fisher Gate remains, near the river bank. It is built of flint and is well preserved.

The tortuous streets of Sandwich have many illustrations of Dutch architecture, due to the number of Flemish weavers who were encouraged by King Edward III to bring the cloth trade to England. They settled in Kent until the industrial revolution encouraged them to take the cloth trade to the north of England. This building is known as The Weavers. Here the weavers specialised in the manufacture of baize and flannels.

Sandwich was at one time a famous port, until like other Cinque Ports it became silted up by the Eastward drift in the Channel. The High Street still goes down to the fine Barbican or Customs House, and the bridge over the River Stour, over which "Berlin chaises" and "calashes", as well as carts and motor cars, had to pay a toll.

In July 1949 the Danes sailed a Viking ship, the "Hugin", across the North Sea, to celebrate the 1500th anniversary of Hengest and Horsa and the Danes' invasion, and the eventual conquest of Britain by the Danes. Today the "Hugin" stands overlooking Pegwell Bay, near Sandwich.

Lady Astor of Hever, wife of the Lord Lieutenant, broke a bottle of champagne on the bow of this £5 million hovercraft at Ramsgate International Hoverport, Pegwell Bay, and named it "Prince of Wales" on June 17, 1977. The band of the Royal Engineers from Chatham played "Life on the Ocean Wave".

Walmer Castle has long been the official residence of the Lord Warden of the Cinque Ports. William Pitt spent some time here, and the Duke of Wellington lived here until his death in 1852. We trust that our new Lord Warden will be able to stay here frequently—at any rate, we hope so.

Deal Castle was erected by King Henry VIII in 1540, together with Walmer Castle and Sandown Castle, as part of his coast defence. Among the Captains of Deal Castle have been the Earl of Ypres (who died here); Lord Allenby; the Marquess of Reading; and Lord Birdwood. Today it is General Sir Norman Tailyour.

Deal Pier, 1000 ft long, was destroyed during the Second World War, when a ship was blown into it. The pier was rebuilt and opened by the Duke of Edinburgh in November 1957. It is a favourite place for sea-fishing competitions.

Near Deal Castle is a tablet which reads "Julius Caesar made his first landing in Britain on Deal Foreshore on August 25th, 55 BC. Finding on his arrival off Dover the armed forces of the British posted on the hills, and the sea so confined by close hills that a dart could be hurled upon the shore", he sailed a few miles from Dover.

This tablet was unveiled on August 25, 1946, by the Mayor of Deal, Councillor Sidney Little, to commemorate the 2000th anniversary of the landing of the Romans.

79

The small church, St Mary's, Barfreston, is a Norman jewel. It is of great antiquity, adorned with carved stone, grotesque heads, circular arches and windows, and surrounded with niches intended for statues. Over the south door is carved Our Lord in Glory, surrounded by many figures, some amusing. Inside, the nave and chancel are separated by a fine Norman arch. There are wreathed pillars and also the remains of frescoes. Above we see the outside of the east end of the church, with its beautiful carved rose window.

Princess Anne in good form on "Mardi Gras" in the Show Jumping section of the Novice Class 2 at Knowlton Horse Trials at Knowlton Court, near Canterbury, in 1974.

Captain Mark Phillips, her husband, won two of the six classes at Knowlton Horse Trials in 1974, winning amongst other prizes a silver rose-bowl and a magnum of champagne. He rode "High Flyer".

AR NEMON WAS ERECTED BY THE ST. MARGARET'S BAY
UNVEILED BY SIR WINSTON CHURCHILL'S GRANDSON
HURCHILL, M.P. ON THE 30TH NOVEMBER 1972

A fine bronze statue of Sir Winston Churchill, sculptured by Oscar Nemon, stands in Pines Garden, St Margaret's at Cliffe. It was erected by St Margaret's Bay Trust, and was unveiled by Sir Winston's grandson, Mr Winston Churchill, MP, on November 30, 1972. The statue was the gift of Mr Frederick Cleary.

The Queen was given a rousing welcome when she visited the Royal Green Jackets and their families at Dover in July 1975.

Duke William, after the Battle of Hastings in 1066, when he met the Men of Kent and Kentish Men at Swanscombe who demanded and received the continuance of their Rights and Privileges, requested in return "the Castel of Dover, with the well of water in it". Here he appointed his half-brother, Odo of Bayeux, as Constable, and made arrangements for its defence. The wall and towers are Norman work. In 1216 the castle was besieged by Louis the Dauphin of France, but Hubert de Burgh refused to capitulate and the castle was spared. The massive Keep was built by Henry II between 1180 and 1186.

The Constable's Tower which forms the main entrance to Dover Castle, has a drawbridge and portcullis. It was built in Henry III's reign.

84

Princess Margaret unveiled a plaque at Dover in 1968 commemorating her visit. She then crossed the Channel in the new 156-ton Mountbatten Class hovercraft, which she steered while crossing the Channel. In this way she inaugurated the hovercraft service between Dover and Boulogne, where she unveiled another plaque. With her on board was Captain Brenna Lund of Dover, Senior Hovercraft Captain of Seaspeed. The Princess lunched at the Casino in Le Touquet.

The Princess looks at a model of the hovercraft on which she travelled.

Princess Anne named the second of British Rail's Seaspeed hovercraft after herself at Dover on Tuesday, October 21, 1969. The Princess unveiled a tablet and then signed a portrait of herself to go on display in the hovercraft terminal building. Afterwards she took a 30-minute trip out to the Goodwin Sands and back. Princess Anne had travelled to Dover from Charing Cross, and was met at Dover Priory by the Mayor and Mayoress, Alderman and Mrs William Muge. The hovercraft cost £1¾m and was built to carry 254 people and 30 cars. After nine years service it was taken to Hampshire and stretched by 56 ft, coming back into operation in July 1978.

Princess Anne meets the members of the crew of "The Princess Anne" at Dover.

"The Princess Anne", the world's largest hovercraft in 1978. Three hundred tons, it carries 416 passengers and 60 cars. In 10 years hovercraft have carried across the Channel 12 million passengers and two million cars.

The White Cliffs of Dover. The chalk cliffs shine white in the sunshine, a sign of happiness and welcome to those returning home. They face the white cliffs of the Pas de Calais to which the White Cliffs of Dover were once joined before the water of the Straits of Dover connected the North Sea with the English Channel.

Where cars enter Dover Harbour Eastern Docks to cross the Straits to the Continent.

The White Cliffs with Dover Castle top left, about which Hubert de Burgh, who was Constable of the Castle in King John's reign, said "Never will I yield to aliens this castle which is the very Key and Gate of England."

Jubilee Way, Dover, which reaches the sea near the Eastern Docks Terminal.

ss "Maid of Kent", which regularly crossed the Channel, in good weather or bad, to Calais, France, before the 1939 War.

The "Maid of Kent" became a hospital ship when war broke out, and was frequently attacked from the air as she crossed to France. Unfortunately she was sunk in 1940.

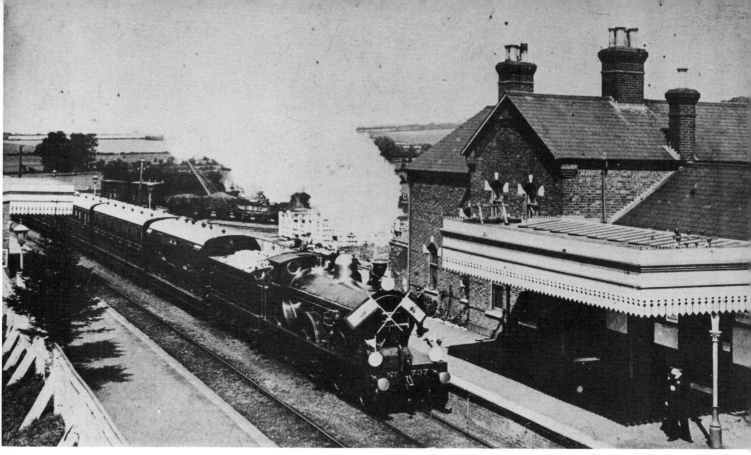

Kent engine "737" or Wainwright D class, was built at Ashford Railway Works, and was described in its day, 1901, as "the most handsome engine ever built". It is taking continental passengers to Dover, and going through Charing Station. When restored it was placed in the British Transport Museum, and when that closed was taken to the Railway Museum in York. Railway men never forget it was Kent built, a grand engine which spent its working life in Kent.

The electric "Golden Arrow" pulling out of Dover Marine Station. After 43 years the last "Golden Arrow" left Victoria for Dover on September 30, 1972.

Townsend Thorensen and Normandy Ferries stand ready to receive passengers and cars in the Eastern Docks. The towers raise and lower the gangway enabling cars and lorries to reach the upper and the lower decks of ships. Townsend and Sealink have placed an £80 million order for five new car ferries. These should be ready in 1980 and will have a capacity for 1000 passengers and 300 cars each.

The Prince of Wales Pier to which is attached the Hoverport landing ground. Seaspeed plans over 8000 flights a year.

This picture of Dover Harbour shows the 10 acre reclamation scheme which has now been completed, and filled with silt, leaving the largest concrete block-laying operation ever to be undertaken in the United Kingdom. It also shows the erection of the £500,000 Export Freight Building at the Eastern Docks.

Admiralty Pier with its Commercial Harbour and Marine Station. Over 8,500,000 passengers passed through the Port of Dover in 1978. Grenville Docks are also seen (bottom left).

It was at Dover, the Clock Tower indeed, that the original Saunders Roe Hovercraft landed in July 1959, after skimming across the Channel from Calais in 2 hours 3 minutes; and 50 years earlier than that, Bleriot flew from Calais to land at Dover in 37 minutes, near the Castle.

The world's largest hovercraft, 300 tons, came into service on the Dover/Boulogne/Calais service in the summer of 1978. It is powered by Rolls Royce Marine Proteus gas turbine engines.

Dover Harbour after the 1939–45 War. Here we see the rail lines on which the "Golden Arrow" took passengers to Admiralty Pier for the cross-Channel boats. The Lord Warden Hotel stands near the entrance to the pier.

Channel Tunnel—yes or no? For over 50 years this question has been discussed. In 1974 digging began in earnest from Shakespeare Cliff, Dover, and this mechanical drilling "mole" was brought in to help. It was made by Robert L. Priestley Ltd. of Gravesend. But by January the following year the scheme was abandoned. The drilling machine has unfortunately been sold. However, cross-Channel traffic has so grown that the tunnel is still wanted by nations on both sides of the Channel.

France began drilling at Sangatte from the French side and made good progress. Here is a view of the tunnel, on the English side, during boring operations.

The division of the ways in the Channel Tunnel. Straight ahead is under Shakespeare Cliff itself, but by turning left you go under the Channel, though only for a short distance, so far.

As the nearest county to the Continent, Kent expects to have traffic crowding its roads. We congratulate Dover especially, as well as Folkestone, Ramsgate and Sheerness, on all they are doing to cope with the cars and container lorries which have increased so rapidly. Regretfully the Channel Tunnel is at present held up. It is needed on both sides of the Channel and when it comes we shall wonder why we did not complete it earlier.

Barham Mill has a long history, for there was a mill here in 1596. It is situated in a good wheat-growing area, and this one was tarred, so it got the name Black Mill on Barham Downs. The mill was built in 1834, and was struck by lightning in 1878. It was claimed to be "the finest mill in Kent and the hardest worker", and had four pairs of stones. In 1970 it was burnt to the ground.

Marshal of the Royal Air Force, Sir William Dickson, unveiled the memorial to the men and women who served at Hawkinge, the nearest aerodrome to the enemy in two World Wars. The memorial was dedicated by the Rev John Chittenden in 1978. The Union Jack is flown upside-down as a sign of distress.

Princess Alexandra (Mrs Angus Ogilvy) opened the new eight-storey Civic Centre in Folkestone on May 4, 1967, when she made her first official visit to the town. She was welcomed by Lord and Lady Cornwallis, and the Mayor (Councillor E. A. Lamb) and civic dignitaries; also the Mayor of Boulogne (M. Henri Henneguelle) and the Burgomaster of Middelburg (Herr Johannes Drijber) and was entertained to lunch at the New Metropole Hotel, before she flew back from Ashford Airport.

The Harvey memorial window above the west door of St Mary and St Eanswythe, Folkestone's Parish Church. It was given by the medical profession in memory of William Harvey who, in 1616, discovered the circulation of the blood. He was born in Church Street, Folkestone.

Troops from all parts of the British Empire marched down the Road of Remembrance at Folkestone on their way to embark on ships in Folkestone Harbour for France during the 1914–18 War, very many thousands never to return.

Nazi bombs falling around Folkestone Harbour, as seen from The Leas near the lifts to the lower promenade. This picture was taken on August 26th, 1940, at the height of the Battle of Britain.

A mural in Folkestone Parish Church, which is named after St Eanswythe, shows St Eanswythe, the daughter of King Eadbald, administering to the poor in AD 630. She devoted herself to the relief of the suffering and distressed, and refused to marry the King of the Northumbrians in order to continue this work.

Birdman Bryan Allen cycled across the English Channel, the first person to do this by leg power, thus earning a £100,000 prize for his team, offered by British Industrialist Henry Kremer. The flight at 10 ft above the sea took two hours and 50 minutes from Folkestone to Cap Gris Nez. His chief problem was to avoid liners and tankers.

Hythe's Town Hall, which dates from 1794. Hythe, as a member of the Confederation of the Cinque Ports, provided one of the Barons who used to carry the canopy over the Sovereign's head at the Coronation. Indeed, in St Leonard's Church there is a stone recalling that the Mayor of Hythe did just this at King James I's coronation. Hythe now forms part of Shepway.

One of the sights to see in Kent is the Hythe Venetian Fete on the Royal Military Canal, when succession after succession of illuminated floats glide by. It makes a very happy evening for competitors and onlookers.

The engine "Dr Syn", pulls out. The small gauge railway was started by Captain J. E. P. Howey on August 24, 1927, from Hythe to New Romney, and was eventually extended to Dungeness. At first it was just a tourists' pleasure trip but today it is an essential link and some 250 schoolchildren travel by it daily.

The only service running in the whole of Britain on January 16, 1979, was the Romney, Hythe and Dymchurch Light Railway, which is under contract to the Kent Education Committee to take students to school at Southlands Comprehensive at New Romney. The special pulled out to time at 8.15 a.m. in spite of the train drivers' strike in the rest of England.

Saltwood Castle, with its fine gateway, was built in the 14th century by Archbishop Courtenay. It was damaged by an earthquake in Queen Elizabeth I's reign. Here Reginald Fitzurse, Hugh de Morville, Richard Brito and William de Tracy, knights of the court of King Henry II, met before they carried out their plan to murder Archbishop à Becket in Canterbury Cathedral on December 29, 1170.

Lympne Castle is a delightful residence, most of which was built in 1907–8. It was added to a 15th-century banqueting hall and tower, which were probably erected on the site of a Roman watch-tower. From it there are magnificent views of the Channel and Romney Marsh, and immediately in front are the remains of Stutfall Castle, or fallen castle, which once guarded the Roman port, Portus Lemanis. Due to the erosion of the chalk cliffs the old Roman castle disintegrated and slid down the cliff. The actual gateway through which the Romans drove their chariots, and parts of the walls, are embedded in the hill.

"Smugglers" carrying the brandy casks ashore to the waiting horses in 1973 during Dymchurch Carnival held in memory of Dr Syn, a Romney Marsh character.

A Dungeness creep, used by the smugglers for retrieving the smuggled brandy casks. If the King's men interrupted their discharge of goods along the coast, the tubs were sunk overboard with long ropes, and these were trawled when the coast was clear, by using the creep.

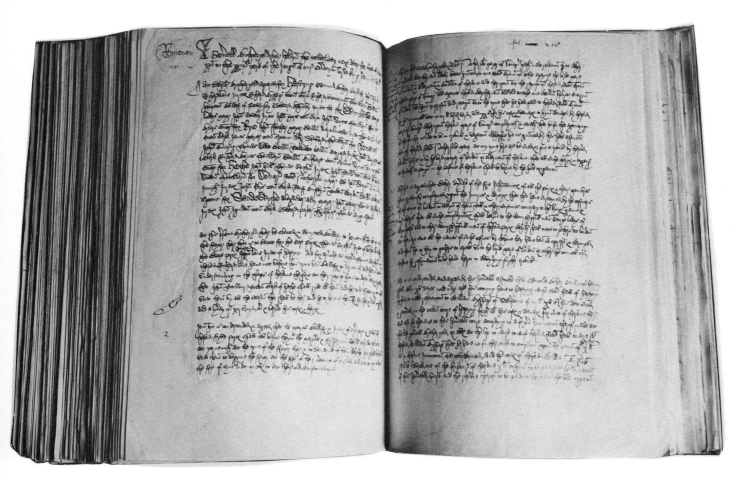

Two pages from the White Book of the Cinque Ports, open at a meeting held in 1531. The minutes of the Brodhull are inscribed for the years 1433 to 1571 in this book, as well as the Canopy Service performed at the Coronations.

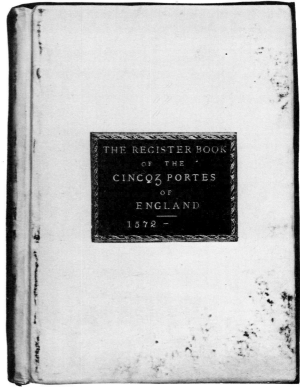

The Register of the Cinque Ports, which is kept in the chest at New Romney, in which the minutes are continued from 1572 until the present time. It also contains the lists of the ships provided by the Cinque Ports.

A typical view on Romney Marsh, sometimes known as the Fifth Continent because it is so different from other parts of England, is one of the most fertile areas. Once under the sea, it has been drained, in sections, down the ages, and today will feed more sheep to the acre than most other parts of Britain.

The Earl of Guilford, President of the Association of Men of Kent and Kentish Men, 1974–1978, invests Miss Anne Roper as the first lady President of the Association of Men of Kent and Kentish Men, and Fair Maids on May 12 1979.

Great changes have taken place on Romney Marsh since the Dungeness Power Station was built, and pylons bring electricity to an area which least expected it 50 years ago, thus making life so much easier, for farmer and housewife.

Lydd Parish Church's Saxon walls, over 1,000 years old, and 13th-century arches, were damaged by Nazi bombs in the Second World War. These have now been repaired. ·

110

Lydd Airport was opened for civil use in 1954, after the 1939–45 War, when the transport of cars was its chief use. Now it is used for passengers and goods by Air Freight Ltd and Dan Air Ltd, and has a local HM Customs. It also has a restaurant which holds 60 people.

The Mayor of Lydd, Councillor Dennis Prior, takes the salute when the Pipes and Drums of the Queen's Own Highlanders Beat Retreat on Lydd Rype in May 1979. The bandsmen also took part in the Wembley Musical Pageant and played at the Berlin Tattoo, Germany, in the same year.

A view of "A" and "B" Station of the General Electricity Generating Board's Power Station at Dungeness, built right on that portion of Kent which juts out into the English Channel. It was from this point that PLUTO—Pipe Line Under The Ocean—pumped motor spirit for the advance of our victorious invasion troops in France in 1944.

The new "B" power station, the first commercial nuclear station in the world to use advanced gas-cooled reactors. The turbine hall contains two 660 MW turbo-generator units.

Fifty years ago the only way to get to Dungeness was to walk over the beach wearing "back stays", a sort of snow shoe on your boots, to prevent sinking into the beach. But it was inhabited by generations of well-known families of fishermen, who still live there, fish and mend their nets.

Local whelks are one of the delicacies of the area, as well as Dover plaice, dabs and mackerel, and many other sorts of fish.

Necessary repairs to the nets and hausers are carried out every day on Dungeness beach.

Since 1820 families have turned out to pull the returning lifeboat ashore over the pebble beach of Dungeness. This is no longer necessary. In October 1978 a new tractor-launched boat, the "Alice Upjohn", came into service.

In 1978 about 300 people saw the £94,000 Dungeness Lifeboat "Alice Upjohn" launched, officially named and dedicated by Lydd Rector, the Rev Peter Chidgey, together with his Roman Catholic and Wesleyan Methodist colleagues, Father Kieran O'Brien and the Rev Dennis Reynolds. The lifeboat was presented to Dungeness Station by Commander Ralph Swann, vice-president of the Royal National Lifeboat Institution, and received by the Station Secretary Mick Bates. Miss Ursula Upjohn, 79 years old, who gave the lifeboat, broke a bottle of champagne on the bows and named her after her mother; she then joined the crew for the launch.

East Kent firemen were airlifted from Lydd Airport in November 1978 to fight a blaze on the Swedish cargo ship "MV Birkaland". The firemen came on board by helicopter with foam equipment and breathing apparatus. The fire was put out in seven hours, but it wrecked the engine room, the captain's quarters and some of the cargo of citrus from Israel.

The old and new lighthouses on Dungeness. The new Dungeness lighthouse was opened by HRH the Duke of Gloucester, the Master of Trinity House, on June 29, 1960.

Ashford Parish Church is dedicated to the Blessed Virgin Mary, and celebrated its 500th anniversary in 1970 when The Queen attended Morning Service. It is cruciform and has a nave with north and south aisles, transepts and three chancels; and a 120 ft tower, which can be seen for miles. It has a clock, eight bells and a set of chimes. A church is mentioned in Ashford in the Domesday Book, 1086. The present edifice is chiefly Decorated and Perpendicular, with some Early English and Norman parts.

Ashford Church chimes used to play during two weeks:

On  Sunday          We love the place, O God.
    Monday          The Harp that once through Tara's Halls.
    Tuesday         God save the Queen.
    Wednesday       Rule Britannia.
    Thursday        A Spanish Chant.
    Friday          Rock of Ages.
    Saturday        Home, sweet Home.

    The week after:
    Sunday          Hanover (the 104th Psalm).
    Monday          Men of Harlech.
    Tuesday         God bless the Prince of Wales.
    Wednesday       Coming thro' the rye.
    Thursday        Ye banks and braes.
    Friday          Abide with me.
    Saturday        The Minstrel Boy.

A peal of bells was hung in 1620 and this set of chimes was installed in 1885. The tunes could be changed.

The Roll of Honour of the Intelligence Corps in St Mary's Parish Church at Ashford. The Corps has been established at Templer Barracks since 1966. The Barracks is named after Field Marshal Sir Gerald Templer. A Corps of Guides was formed in Kent in 1801 when Napoleon was expected to invade Kent.

This fine rood screen in St Mary's Church, Ashford, is a memorial to all those from Ashford District who gave their lives in the 1914–1918 War. It was erected in 1920.

Lord Astor of Hever, Lord Lieutenant of Kent, presented on behalf of the Queen, the grant of arms which officially marked Ashford's status as a Borough, on Monday, November 29, 1976. It was received by the third Mayor of Ashford, Councillor Harry Watts, who rightly called the event "a momentous occasion in Ashford's history".

To celebrate the occasion a rousing Fanfare was sounded by trumpeters of the Royal Greenjackets, in Norton Knatchbull School, in salute to the new Borough of Ashford.

Prince Philip went with Lord Brabourne, the president, to the Ashford Fat Stock Show. Ashford has always been a centre for farmers in East Kent and on Romney Marsh.

He presented the prizes to the winners at the 100th Ashford Fat Stock Show on December 16, 1968.

The Intelligence Corps received the Freedom of the Borough of Ashford on May 16, 1979. The Chief Executive, Mr Ernest Mexter read the scroll and the Mayor, Major W. Cotton, presented the casket to Lieutenant-General Sir Michael Gow, the Colonel-Commandant of the Corps. The Corps then marched through Ashford High Street with bayonets fixed, led by the Band of the Royal Engineers.

The arrival in August 1919 of the tank, which still stands in St George's Square, Ashford, was preceded by a military band, Wolf Cubs and Scouts. The tank chugged its way through massed crowds from Ashford Station yard. Described as "a Mark iv Female", it was driven by a 105 hp four-stroke, slieve valve Daimler engine. It carried a crew of eight: an officer, NCO, and six men, with the tank colours of brown, red and green, standing for "Through mud, through blood, to the green fields of Peace".

The Ashford Heritage Centre in Hythe Road was officially opened by the Mayor of Ashford, Councillor Brian Prebble, in February 1978. It houses thousands of photographs of Ashford and Kent, and has Kent's first Victorian Living Museum, four rooms having been set aside and used as they would have been used in times past.

The stately home, Eastwell Park, which stands in a 2,600 acre estate, was bought in 1977 by Thomas Bates and Son. Planning permission has been sought to turn it into a luxury hotel. Originally it was a manor house and was built by Hugo de Montfort and extended by Thomas Moyle in 1546, when a bricklayer, believed to be the son of King Richard III, was employed; he is buried in the ruined Eastwell Church. Eastwell Park was the property of the Earls of Winchelsea for 300 years, during which both Queen Victoria and King Edward VII were visitors. Viscountess Midleton bought it in 1928.

Godmersham Park where Jane Austen stayed with her brother Edward Knight and wrote about, with such enjoyment. It has one of the most beautiful parks in Kent.

Chilham Castle was built in 1616 by Sir Dudley Digges. There is also an old Roman Keep, for the Romans fought battles here when the Britons vigorously defended the River Stour. The Saxon King Withred of Kent, 649–725, lived in this stronghold.

Bilsington Women's Institute celebrated its 50th anniversary in June 1979. Among those near the table are the East Kent Chairman, Mrs M. Wigfall (left), Mrs E. M. Boorman, Miss Owen, Mrs Stanger, Mrs Fanshawe (the President), Mrs Russell, Mrs Dobell and Mrs Elford. It is Mrs Daw cutting the cake, who joined the Women's Institute at its foundation, when 17 years old. The Women's Institutes have done so much especially for the villages in our county.

A major hospital for south-east Kent has been opened at Ashford. It is the William Harvey Hospital, named after the physician who was born in Folkestone in 1578, where there is a West window in his memory in the Parish Church. The hospital will have 680 beds and is a centre for medical training and education.

One of the relics—part of a Stuka dive-bomber—on display at the Battle of Britain Museum at Chilham Castle, being shown by Tony Webb. The Curator, Mike Llewellyn, hopes to find larger premises for the Museum.

There are dene-holes in many parts of Kent, due to the chalk. Some of these in East Kent are believed to have been used as hiding places both for worship and, more recently, by smugglers. Many have now been filled in. This one is at Challock.

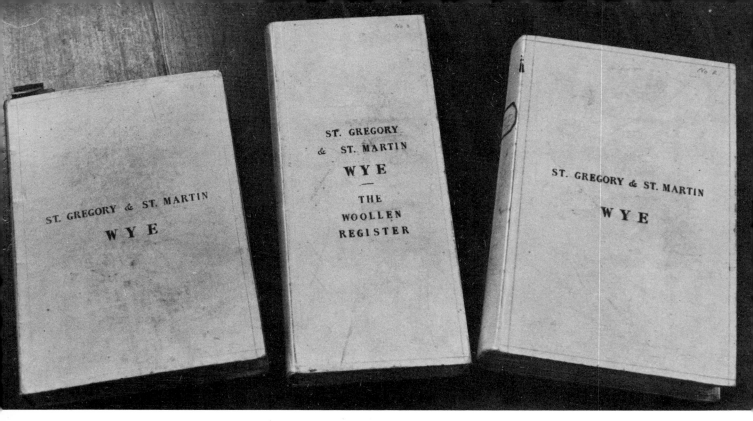

The registers of St Gregory and St Martin, Wye, are of great interest. The marriage register goes back to 1654. It is, however, the Woollen Register, which is of special interest.

The Woollen Register at Wye shows that when burials were carried out, bodies were wrapped in wool to encourage the cloth industry and the Flemish weavers brought to this country by Edward III. An entry in 1678:

"August 17. Richard Epsley of Wye was then buried on the 14th day of the same month, received a certificate under the hand and seal of Sir Thomas Buss: two witnesses had taken their oathes before him that the above named was buried in sheep's wool only, according to the late Act of Parliament.

August 23. Richard Brett of Willesborough . . . buried in the Church on the 27th day of the same month.

October 14th. Elizabeth Brissenden was then buried on the 19th day of the same month, received a certificate under the hand of Sir Will Honeywood . . . that the above named party, deceased, was buried in sheep's wool only, altogether according to the late Act of Parliament to that purpose . . .

Richard Banks was then buried on the 23rd day of the same month, received a certificate under the hand of Herbert Randolph Esq., one of the Justices of the Peace for the County of Kent: oath was made before him that the above named was buried in sheep's wool only according to the late Act of Parliament, to that purpose . . ."

1678:

August ye
7: 14th day of ye same moneth, & rec:d ... Richard Epsley of Wye was then bur... ... under ye hand & Seale of Sr ...

The entry of Richard Epsley of Wye and Richard Brett of Willesborough.

Also Elizabeth Brissenden and Richard Banks.

The old houses in Biddenden, some of which were left by the Biddenden Maids, Eliza and Mary Chaulkhurst, twins born joined together by their arm and thigh. The rents pay for the bread and biscuits which are distributed to parishioners every Easter. Note the pavement of Bethersden Marble.

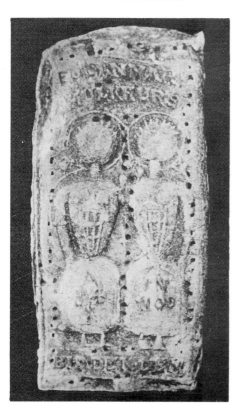

The distribution of bread and biscuits to pensioners and visitors on Easter Monday.

A Biddenden biscuit.

Even in the rain they queue to receive the ration of bread, cheese and biscuits, from the Chaulkhurst Charity every Easter—visitors as well.

The ancient pavement composed of durable Bethersden Marble, once so useful in the wet clay soil of the Weald of Kent.

Biddenden Spectacular, the exciting annual fair organised each year by the village of Biddenden.

A balloon ascends at Biddenden Spectacular.

An old picture showing the toll-gate which was at one time erected in the centre of Tenterden in order to maintain the roads in this wealthy town.

Tenterden, since 1975 linked with growing Ashford, and a Limb of the Cinque Ports, was incorporated in 1448, the only corporate town in the Weald of Kent. In times past Tenterden had its own port at Smallhythe, where the 400 ton "the Grand Master" was built. There is also the legend that the tower of the Church of St Mildred was the cause of the Goodwin Sands. Tenterden owed its growth and prosperity to the broadcloth manufactured and taught by the Flemish weavers. Legend has it that the Abbot used stone to build the church tower which should have been used to maintain the sea wall.

A former club president, Sir Alexander Sim, opened Tenterden's new Golf Clubhouse in the presence of 100 people, one of whom was another past president, Mr John Major, in May 1979. The guests were welcomed by the Club Captain, Bob Foster.

Zion Baptist Church in Tenterden High Street was opened in 1835, and rebuilt and extended to celebrate Queen Victoria's Golden Jubilee in 1887.

In 1976 the Mayor of Tenterden, Councillor Hugh Roberts, and the Council, welcomed the Master and members of the Worshipful Company of Stationers and Newspapers Makers, who visited Tenterden when an exhibition of Caxton's works was held, including the Polychronicon, a valuable book owned by Tenterden Council and printed by Caxton in 1482. It is believed that Caxton, who introduced the art of printing to England, was born in Tenterden.

The light railway between Headcorn, Tenterden and Robertsbridge, which had been closed, was re-opened by local enthusiasts in 1977. It runs from Tenterden to Bodiam. With Union Jacks flying No 10 breaks the ribbon across the bridge.

137

One of the rural causeways in the Weald of Kent, mentioned by William Cobbett in his ''Rural Rides''. To enable pack horses to take wool and cloth, made by the Kent weavers, to market, these historic pathways of durable Bethersden Marble were laid on the heavy clay soil, which was almost impassable in bad weather. This pathway linked Tenterden with Rolvenden.

With plumes on their backs, two fine Shire horses plough some of the most productive land in Kent during a Ploughing Match in 1977 at Marden.

Smarden, looking up the picturesque High Street from the village well.

The Cloth Hall, Smarden, was a centre for Flemish Weavers making broadcloth 500 years ago. They were known as the Grey Coats of Kent, from their undyed woollen overcoats. Note the hook for raising the bales of wool.

White clapboard houses, as well as the Canterbury Bell Inn, make Sandhurst such a pleasing village to visit.

The Baptist Chapel at Sandhurst, to which in times past farmers drove their pony traps from miles around on Sunday mornings. They stabled their horses in the stables at the rear of the chapel. Now these stables are Sunday School rooms and, of course, most of the congregation comes by car.

A corner in Cranbrook, a town which takes its name from the Crane Brook. It became the centre for the Flemish Weavers who came to Kent at the invitation of Edward III. Here the first cloth was made, and Queen Elizabeth I walked a mile from the George Hotel to Coursehorne, one of the Cloth Halls, on grey cloth made from Romney Marsh sheep.

Cranbrook School has a long and interesting history. It started as a Free School in the reign of Queen Elizabeth I, when Simon Lynch gave a house and land in Cranbrook called "Blueberry" to which was added 123 acres at Horsmonden. However, the parishioners complained because dead languages like Latin and Greek were taught, when they said so few had use for these languages!

The Union Mill, a fine specimen of a Kent smock mill, towers over Cranbrook; it is 70 ft tall. It is said that when the mill was built in 1814, the builder's son stood on the cap and blew a bugle to celebrate the completion.

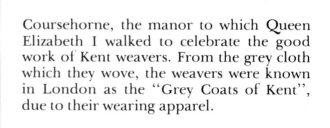

Coursehorne, the manor to which Queen Elizabeth I walked to celebrate the good work of Kent weavers. From the grey cloth which they wove, the weavers were known in London as the "Grey Coats of Kent", due to their wearing apparel.

143

The Flemish Weavers brought with them hops and also the hop oasts with their cowls on top, such a feature of the Kent countryside. Today most hops are picked by machine, and many of the oasts are now being turned into private houses.

Kent is noted for its fruit—strawberries, raspberries, cherries and apples. More apple orchards are being planted all over Kent. An apple a day keeps the doctor away!

Lady Astor of Hever, accompanied by Lord Astor, the Lord Lieutenant of Kent, opened the £75,000 Art Wing at Bethany School, Goudhurst, in April 1978. She is seen with her husband and Mr Mark Ward, left, Director of Art, examining the pictures exhibited.

The 14th-century tower of Scotney Castle, Lamberhurst, in its delightful setting, overlooking a lake and surrounded by azaleas and rhododendrons.

In the chancel of the handsome Church of St Margaret, Horsmonden, is the brass of Robert de Groshurst in ecclesiastical vestments. He founded a perpetual chantry here. The church is 1½ miles from the village. Another well-known family is the Smith-Marriott, who were patrons and incumbents, as well as Lords of the Manor of Horsmonden, with the patronage of the church being attached to the manor. The large rectory is surrounded by a spacious park.

A rubbing of a fine brass of Henry de Groshurst, rector, 1311–1361, of St Margaret's Church, Horsmonden. It shows him in his full vestments.

146

There are several iron grave slabs in Kent, cast by local furnaces when the Weald of Kent was the centre of the iron industry. These two are in the churchyard at Cowden. They show craftsmanship at its best.

Kent has many double- and single-headed tombstones, some of them with curious images, as at West Peckham.

Prince Charles, Patron of the Men of the Trees, planted a tree, helped by Mr Ben Tompsett, at his residence Chevening Place in 1977. Chevening Place, Kent, stands in 250 acres. The centre was built by Inigo Jones about 1625, the wings were added in 1721. For three centuries it was the residence of the Lennard family, when it was sold to Major-General James Stanhope, who was the first Earl Stanhope. In 1959 it was vested by Lord Stanhope in the State by Act of Parliament. We in Kent are glad that the Prince of Wales has taken up residence here.

Princess Anne planted a tree after opening the £62,500 Sixth Form block and Staff Room at Benenden School in 1970. She was a pupil until 1968. With her at the opening ceremony was the Headmistress, Miss Elizabeth Clarke, and Dame Annis Gillie, the Chairman of the School Council.

HM Queen Elizabeth, The Queen Mother, plants a tree at Walmer Castle to commemorate her acceptance of the invitation to become the first lady Lord Warden of the Cinque Ports, 1979.

The Earl of Aylesford (right) planted a tree to commemorate the Queen's Silver Jubilee, in the sandpit at Aylesford, and unveiled a plaque in October 1977.

To replace some of the elm trees lost by Dutch disease, the Men of the Trees encouraged trees to be planted all over Kent throughout the 70s. Mr Donald Sykes (Wye College bursar), Mr Ian Reid (director of the college's Centre for European Studies), Mrs P. Stevens, Mr Tim Day, and Mr Alan Smith of the Kent Men of the Trees, planted a tree at Wye College on November 13, 1978.

Another planting took place at Grafty Green to celebrate the Queen's Silver Jubilee in 1977.

Mrs Freda Dowling, the president of the Invicta Luncheon Club, whose main aim is friendship, planted a tree on the bank of the River Medway on the Jubilee River Walk, Maidstone, in November 1977. With her were Mrs Margaret Golding-Wood, chairman; Mrs Pat Harden, secretary; and committee members Mrs Brenda Ormerod and Mrs Hilary Harding.

Dr T. H. E. Taylor, president of the Tenterden Trust, watches Amanda Willgrave and Simon Barton (holding spades) plant a tree in November 1977 in Glebe Field, Tenterden, to add to those planted in past years by children of the Junior School.

The Friends of Lydd planted trees near All Saints Church and outside the pensioners' flats at Mittell Court. Among the trees planted are Cherry, Maple, Mountain Ash and a "Tree of Heaven". Mr Philip Puxty is seen covering the roots.

As part of the scheme by the Kent Men of the Trees to replace the lost trees in Kent, Mrs Ann Kyne, chairman of the Ecology Section of Yalding and Nettlestead Protective Society, plants a tree at Yalding in November 1977.

Lord Astor, the Lord Lieutenant of Kent, helped children to plant seven trees in New Romney as part of the scheme in which the Cinque Ports, namely Hastings, Sandwich, Dover, Hythe and New Romney, planted seven trees each to commemorate the 700th anniversary of the Confederation's Great Charter of the Cinque Ports on November 14, 1978—the 30th birthday of Prince Charles, patron of the Men of the Trees. The seven trees at Hastings were planted by Lord Abergavenny.

Mrs Peggy Stevens, chairman of the Kent Men of the Trees, plants a Prunus Pink Perfection tree outside the Sea Bathing Hospital at Margate in 1977.

Tonbridge Castle is really the gateway to the castle, which was built by the Norman, Richard de Tonbridge, uncle of William I, who created him Earl of Clare.

The Prime Minister, Mr Edward Heath, enjoyed opening the Tonbridge By-pass in July 1971. He is seen cutting the tape which is held by the chairman of the Kent County Roads Committee, Alderman W. Simmons. With them is the Bishop of Rochester, Dr Richard Say.

The construction of the A26 (Tunbridge Wells to Sevenoaks road) which by-passes Tonbridge. Quarry Hill joins it near Baltic Road. The white building is Modeluxe Linen Services, which is approached by Woodlands Road, and on the left is the car park of Redland Brick Works.

Over the gateway at Penshurst Place is an inscription which tells us "That most religious and renowned Prince Edward the Sixth, Kinge of England, France and Ireland, bestowed Penshurst upon his trusty and well-beloved Sir William Sydney, who had served from the tyme of his birth unto his coronation in the offices of Chamberlayn and Steward of his Household." Philip Sidney, Kent's bard who wrote the pastoral romance "Arcadia", was born here, and today Lord De L'Isle, who in 1944 won the VC on Anzio Beach, is a descendant and lives here.

In Penshurst Place, Queen Elizabeth I danced with Dudley in the fine baronial hall, and the Black Prince dined at Christmas with Joan, the Fair Maid of Kent.

Royal Tunbridge Wells Council offices have an Assembly Hall with a Library, Museum, and a Police Station adjoining. The Wells were discovered by Dudley, Lord North, in 1606. Queen Henrietta Maria found the waters beneficial in 1630, and many people have tried the cure at the wells in the Pantiles. Defoe wrote that "any gentleman of decency and good manners may talk with any lady" at this resort of fashion and beauty.

The new reservoir at Bough Beech, near Edenbridge, which has a capacity of 2000 million gallons, was ready in 1969. It has a dam 4,000 ft long, and 80 ft from the bottom of the reservoir to the top, built of Weald clay. Six houses were lost in the flooding, but two were dismantled and re-erected on the West Dean Estate, near Chichester. Water will be pumped from the River Eden through a 49-inch pipe, and some water will also be supplied by Bough Beech Brook.

Lady Astor accompanied Lord Cornwallis to the saluting base when the Royal British Legion attended a service at Hever Castle on July 10, 1971. This was one of the last duties carried out by Lord Cornwallis as Lord Lieutenant of Kent, for he retired as Her Majesty's representative in Kent on July 31, 1972, after 28 years of splendid service to both The Queen and Kent. He is known as "The Spirit of Kent".

In 1978, Lord Astor of Hever, Lord Lieutenant of Kent since 1972, on behalf of HM The Queen, presented the British Empire Medal to Miss Vera Gilchrist Thompson of Tonbridge, at Hever Castle, for her services to Kent Red Cross. With them are Mr Philip Tedham of Lamberhurst (left) who received the BEM for his work at the Post Office, and Captain Percy Mackenzie of Bidborough (right), who received the Queen's Commendation for service in the air.

There were 4,000 members at the Royal British Legion service at Hever Castle, which was conducted by the Bishop of Tonbridge, Dr H. D. Halsey, on July 10, 1971. It was the Golden Jubilee of the Legion's foundation by Earl Haig (Lady Astor's father). The march-past salute was taken by Lord Cornwallis.

The massed banners of Kent branches of the Royal British Legion, at the service.

On the Green at Westerham, a spot the late Sir Winston Churchill often passed, Sir Robert Menzies, the Lord Warden of the Cinque Ports, 1966–1978, unveiled a bronze statue of Sir Winston on July 23, 1969, in gratitude for his defiance and leadership during the 1939–45 War—a fitting statue (sculptured by Oscar Nemon) to stand with General Wolfe who captured Quebec.

The monument erected at Westerham in memory of another hero, Major-General James Wolfe, killed in action at the capture of Quebec, Canada. He was born at Parsonage House and later lived in Quebec House in Westerham.

Stags graze happily in the 1,000-acre park outside Knole, Sevenoaks, a 15th-century treasure house now maintained by the National Trust and visited by thousands of people every year. It belonged to the Sackville family. Archbishop Bouchier built most of the present structure, and Archbishop Warham built the gatehouse of this historic building.

The Cartoon Gallery, Knole, Sevenoaks, named from the six copies traditionally associated with Daniel Mytens and Raphael's cartoons. They were brought to Knole by Frances, the wife of the fifth Earl of Dorset. Apart from the cartoons this gallery has a fine plaster ceiling, a marble mantelpiece, Jacobean woodwork and furniture of Charles II period in green, blue and crimson Genoa velvet.

161

The Queen, together with Prince Philip, Duke of Edinburgh, in 1972 paid a visit to the Royal Armament Research and Development Establishment at Fort Halstead. The Queen is speaking to the apprentice of the year, Graham Ayers of Sidcup, aged 21. Prince Philip chats with Brian Clough of Swanley, aged 19. On the left is Mr F. H. East, the Director.

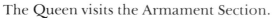

The Queen visits the Armament Section.

Princess Anne signs the visitors' book after opening the £500,000 Out-Patients' Wing at West Hill Hospital, Dartford, in 1971, where crowds welcomed her on arrival. With her is the Mayor of Dartford, Councillor Albert May.

Princess Anne chats with Caroline McLellan, aged 13, one of the patients at the Joyce Green Hospital, and her friends, during her visit to Dartford on November 8, 1971.

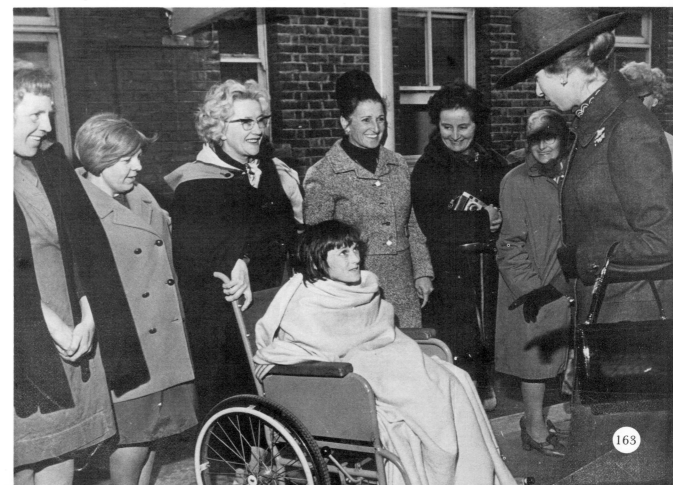

The "Bridge to Nowhere", so far! To reduce the cost of bridge-building it is much cheaper to build three bridges at the same time—provided, of course, they are all needed, but what if there are demonstrations and enquiries against the third? This is what has happened at Swanley. The M25 Swanley to Sevenoaks link, has been held up because it would spoil Samuel Palmer's "Valley of Vision", the Darenth Valley.

The Thames as seen from the Royal Clarendon Hotel, Gravesend. Nearby is the waterside Church of St Andrew, built north to south, instead of east to west, due to lack of space. Here the baptismal registers date from 1864 and contain the names of emigrants, whole families indeed, who were baptised as their ships lay off Gravesend, before leaving for the Dominions and Colonies. The church bells were rung in farewell as each emigrant ship sailed down the Thames.

The Duchess of Kent opened Gravesend's £1 million Civic Centre on November 15, 1968, in the presence of the mayor, Alderman Charles Suter, and Lord Cornwallis, then Lord Lieutenant of Kent. The Centre was dedicated by the Bishop of Rochester, Dr Richard Say.

The Duchess of Kent talks to some of the schoolchildren who came to see her open the new Civic Centre at Gravesend (now called Gravesham with the additional areas of Northfleet Urban District Council and part of Strood Rural District Council).

The Minister of Energy, The Rt Hon Eric Varley, officially opened the Kingsnorth (Isle of Grain) Power Station in 1975. This £113 million power station is the only oil and coal fired power station in Britain, and the biggest in Europe. With an output of 2,000 megawatts the station can produce sufficient electricity for a city of two million people. The power is fed into the National Grid.

Mr Eric Varley is shown the turbo alternators generating the power of 23,500 volts. These are fed into large transformers which raise the voltage to 400,000 volts.

The first church at Rochester was dedicated to the honour of God and the apostle St Andrew, and was built about 604 AD. It existed until about 1080, when Bishop Gundulph rebuilt the present noble cruciform structure, including nave with aisles, choir and transepts, with a tower, which form the Cathedral today. From West door to the steps into the choir it is 150 ft, and from the steps to the Altar another 156 ft. The cross aisle at the choir is 122 ft, and another cross aisle between the High Altar and the Bishop's throne, north to south, is 90 ft.

To the west, close by, is Rochester Castle, whose massive keep is 70 ft square, with walls about 11 to 13 ft thick, and 100 ft high including the embattlements. The ditch which surrounded the castle on three sides has been filled, with the River Medway on the fourth side. The keep is built of Kentish Rag, cemented with quantities of shells. It has a draw-bridge to the lower apartments. A 5 ft staircase ascends to the top past four storeys.

The nave of Rochester Cathedral is one of the best examples of Norman work; the clerestory and the roof are of Perpendicular period. Ahead is the screen under the organ, with figures of St Andrew, King Ethelbert, St Justus, St Paulinus, Bishop Gundulph, William de Hoo, Bishop Walter de Merton and Cardinal John Fisher.

Dr R. D. Say was enthroned the 104th Bishop of Rochester on January 29, 1961. He is seen giving the Blessing on the steps of the Cathedral nave at the conclusion of the service.

The Queen distributed the Maundy Money to 70 old people in Rochester Cathedral on March 30, 1961, when she and Prince Philip visited Rochester. They are seen leaving the cathedral with the Dean, the Rt Rev R. W. Stannard, and the Bishop, Dr Richard Say. The pavements were crowded as they arrived at the Guildhall where the Mayor, Councillor I. J. Phillips, presented the Loyal Address, and showed The Queen the City's charters. After lunch in the Corn Exchange The Queen addressed the citizens in the Castle gardens, thanking them for their warm welcome and loyalty. She said she was glad to visit Rochester during the 500th anniversary of their charter, which raised their predecessor to the dignity of Mayor. It was a happy day.

The Bishop with the Chapter of Rochester Cathedral and the clergy who attended the enthronement.

169

The Catalpa Tree outside Rochester Cathedral. It is grown from an Indian Bean which is indigenous to North America, the West Indies and also Eastern Asia. No-one knows who planted it 100 years ago in this beautiful spot.

Choristers of Rochester Cathedral singing in the Crypt or Undercroft. Altars down here were dedicated to St Katherine, St Mary Magdalene, St Michael, Holy Trinity, St Edmund and St Denis.

The beautiful west door and window of the Cathedral are of great interest. The columns round the west door have statues, two of whom were Bishop Gundulph's royal patrons, King Henry I and his Queen Matilda. The keystone shows Our Saviour sitting with raised hand in benediction, and a book in the other hand. Inside the Cathedral is a memorial recalling Charles Dickens, the novelist, who died at Gads Hill Place in 1870.

The Mayor of Rochester, Alderman E. Washford, gives a wave as the stage coach, carrying Rochester Dickensians in costume, repeated Mr Pickwick's famous ride from the Bull Hotel, Rochester, to Dingley Dell at Cobtree, near Maidstone.

"Mr Pickwick" (Mr F. M. Kendall) and the Pickwick Club drive round the ring in their coach at the Cobham Cricket Club Centenary celebrations in 1950.

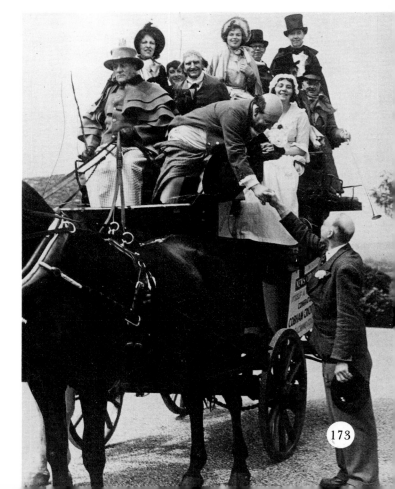

"Mr Pickwick" and the Pickwick Club are welcomed to Dingley Dell (Cobtree Manor) by Sir Garrard Tyrwhitt-Drake.

Picturesque craft jostle for position in the Stay Sail class in the Barge Race in 1950. The Barge Race was started in 1863 by William Dodd.

"Sirdir" goes in the opposite direction! She made a false start and went over a mile before she had to turn back. In spite of starting last, 17 minutes late, in 1950, she won the Medway Barge Race.

The River Medway twists and bends as it passes the village of Wouldham, which was given by Ethelbert, King of Kent, to the Church of St Andrew in Rochester in 751 AD. The existence of a church at Wouldham was noted in the Domesday Book. The lychgate was erected in memory of 41 men who gave their lives in the First World War.

The River Medway straightens as it passes Malling Precast Ltd on the east bank (left of picture), at the back of which is Rugby Portland Cement. Close by is the famous Horseshoe Bend in the river.

A view of Snodland with Rectory Close, Ham Hill, in the foreground, the cricket ground in the centre of the picture, and Holborough Cement Works at the top.

Around Blue Bell Hill on the chalk Downs we see an area which has been called Grey Wethers. In this area there are stone circles, single stones and grey stones in groups, believed to be associated with Druid sites. They are scattered around the hillside like sheep. No doubt in time this area will be explored on a national scale.

In the distance is Aylesford and its paper mills bordering the River Medway. The area between Maidstone and the North Downs is known as the Medway Gap, an area which is developing rapidly; indeed, it is an area to which industry, attracted to the south-east to export goods to Europe, will be directed, together with housing estates for the workers.

The Duke of Kent, vice-chairman of the Board of Trade, visited Reed's paper mill at Aylesford, where he met the group chairman, "Squire" Wilkins, and toured the multi-million pound de-inking plant, after he had opened St Peter's Bridge in Maidstone, on November 23, 1978. With him is Lord Astor of Hever, the Lord Lieutenant.

Dame Sybil Thorndike, the famous actress, in her 90th year on July 30, 1972, opened a Community Centre in Aylesford (the village on the River Medway in which she was born and also married), amidst the applause of her many friends.

A beautiful picture of old and new. Kits Coty, as old as Stonehenge, stands framed by the new leaves of Spring. What was this historic monument, belonging to the New Stone Age when the inhabitants lived in settlements, tilled the soil and kept cattle? Some believe Kits Coty was the entrance to a burial mound or tumulus, perhaps of a chieftain, and the soil has gradually eroded leaving only the stones. Some say it is an altar used by the Druids, some that the stones denote where there is water. Perhaps it is all. There are many other stones and circles near Blue Bell Hill. Some day the area will be carefully excavated, and will yield many interesting secrets of past ages.

The Carmelite Fathers now have a conference centre at Allington Castle, which was built by Stephen de Penchester in 1282. Sir Thomas Wyatt who introduced the sonnet into English verse was born here in 1503. Because of his love for Anne Boleyn, Henry VIII's second wife, he was imprisoned in the Tower of London. Allington is a popular place of call for those on the River Medway. The Prior of the Carmelite Fathers is at Aylesford priory.

Wateringbury is another happy area for those on the River Medway, and also for caravans. It is in a delightful part of Kent between Maidstone and Tonbridge, which due to the fertile loam is very productive for corn, fruit and hops. Long discontinued, a Court was held in Chart garden at which a deputy to the Dumb Borsholder of Chart was elected, to whom was given certain liberties. The Dumb Borsholder itself hangs in the Church of St John the Baptist at Wateringbury.

Kingsferry Bridge, the Isle of Sheppey's vital link with the mainland, was opened by HRH Princess Marina, the Duchess of Kent, on April 20, 1960.

Queenborough in Sheppey was named a free borough by King Edward III in honour of his Queen, Philippa. He granted a staple for wool, gave the town a Mayor, fairs, weekly markets and other privileges. The Mayor's wand of office is an olive branch from Palestine, and the silver gilt mace is dated 1668. The Guildhall, shown here, was built in the 18th century. In Queenborough at Church House resided Lady Hamilton, whom Lord Nelson regularly visited when he lived at 149 High Street, Sheerness.

Prince Philip opened the Sheerness Steel Company's steelworks on the Isle of Sheppey in 1972. He is seen with Sir Charles Wheeler, the chairman (left); Lord Astor; and the Mayor of Queenborough, Alderman Richard Sharrock (right).

Great changes are taking place at Sheerness. The building on the right, the Quadrangular Storehouse, built in 1829 is being demolished. At one time it was the largest storehouse in the country. This part was known as Powder Monkey Bay, where the gunpowder was kept. The 19th-century clock tower is to be preserved. To give more room for trade, the smaller docks are to be filled. Sheerness is a noted centre for roll-on, roll-off traffic, also for container-transport and passengers.

190

The figurehead of HMS "Forte", the last commissioned flagship of the East Indies, paid off in 1872 and burnt at Sheerness on November 23, 1908, stands outside the Medway Ports Authority headquarters.

The Medway Ports Authority controls the estuary of the River Medway, the River Swale and as far up-stream as Maidstone. This area includes the docks at Sheerness and the wharves at Queenborough, Rochester and Rainham. It took over control from the Medway Conservancy in October 1969. The Royal Dockyard of Sheerness was established in 1665.

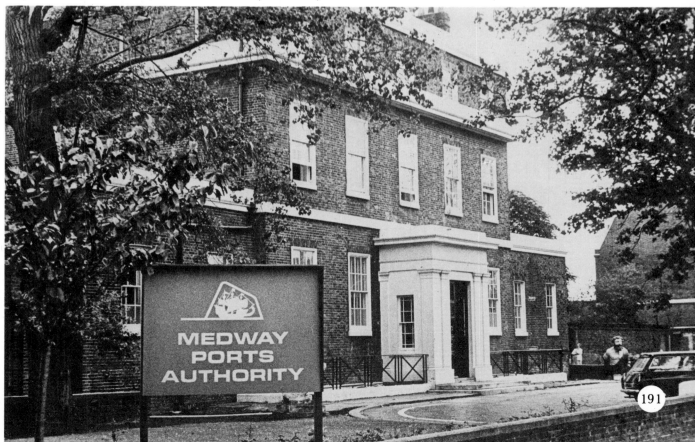

Garrison Point where the River Medway meets the River Thames. The fort, a solid structure, was built in 1860. Today it is used for radar. In port is a ship of the Olau-Line ferry. Already Sheerness is important for the import of cars, bananas, beef and wine, and also for the export of Leyland cars and other freight.

Sheerness Passenger Terminal, used by passengers on the Olau-Line ferries. 500,000 passengers crossed the Channel from Sheerness in 1978.

The car compound for hundreds of cars at Queenborough where the foreign cars which land at Sheerness are stored after they have passed Customs. Mike Steel (left) and Errol Cox of Bluett Shipping are seen amongst the cars. Among the cars imported are the Honda, Polski, Fiat, Toyota, Mazda and Wartburg.

The Clock Tower, Sheerness, has been in the High Street ever since it was built by public subscription to celebrate the Coronation of King Edward VII. Few people in the past noticed it, except just to check their watches, so because of the growth in traffic it was decided to move it to the station. But there was such a public uproar, that the Council only moved it to one side of the road.

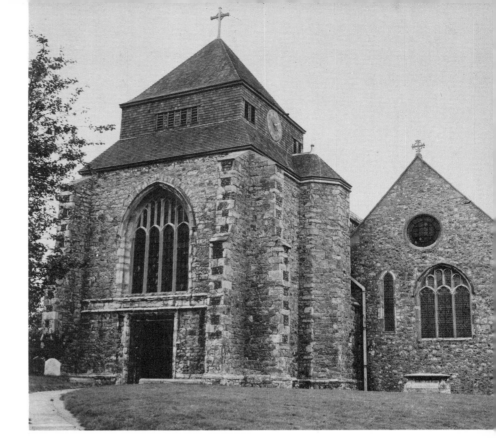

S·SEXBVRGA QUEEN & ABBESS

St Sexburga, widow of Ercombert, King of Kent, founded the convent at Minster, Sheppey, for nuns of the Benedictine Order in AD 664. The abbey was large and wealthy, but was burnt down by the Danes and also by Earl Godwin. The abbey and church were rebuilt in 1130, but the abbey was suppressed by Henry VIII. The church today is believed to be two churches, the North Church being the church of the abbey, which had the Nuns Chapel screened off. The tower was built in the 15th century.

The winter of January to March 1979 was one of the worst on record. In Kent most roads were kept open, except for a night or two when motorists could not get ahead because of the vehicles abandoned by the roadside. Airfields were snowbound, and in the north of England some parts were 20 ft deep in snow. The police urged everyone to remain in their homes unless they could be sure of reaching their destinations. This is a picture of Cobham Church during one of the earlier snowfalls.

Sukam, a Siberian tiger, an exhibit at Port Lympne Wildlife Sanctuary, enjoys a good meal in the wintry weather in January 1979.

The six Siberian huskies delight to pull Mr Joe Griffin's sleigh at Mount Farm Hothfield.

In the Siberian tiger sanctuary at Port Lympne, eight tiger cubs have been born, four of them to Sukam and Guglia. In this picture Sukam is taking two of the cubs to water, but no-one can force them to drink!

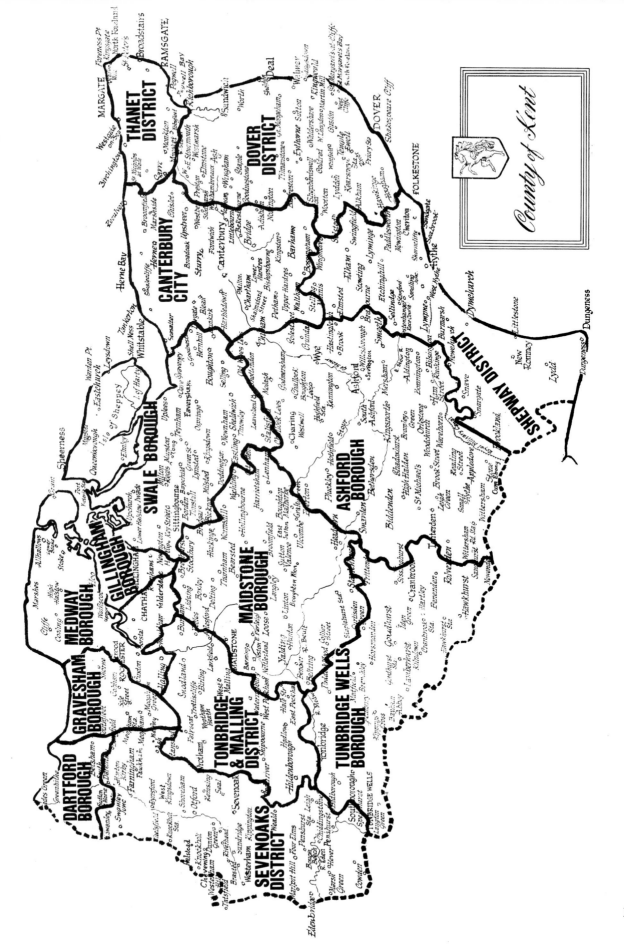

County of Kent

# INDEX